PRAISE FOR

MAEVE RISING

"Maeve DuVally, whom I used to know as Michael DuVally from Goldman Sachs, has written a courageous and compelling memoir about her literal and metaphorical transformation, from a man to a woman, from drunkenness to sobriety, from a life filled with lies and deceit, to one of honesty and openness. What an inspiring story."

—WILLIAM D. COHAN, *author of Power Failure: The Rise and Fall of an American Icon; Money and Power: How Goldman Sachs Came to Rule the World; House of Cards: A Tale of Hubris and Wretched Excess on Wall Street; and, The Last Tycoons: The Secret History of Lazard Frères & Co*

. . . . . .

"This is Maeve DuVally's heartbreaking, brave, and triumphant story of coming out as a transgender person not just in corporate America, but on Wall Street, and not just on Wall Street, but at Goldman Sachs. It would be important reading at any time, but in the times in which we live, it's essential."

—BETHANY MCLEAN, *co-author of The Smartest Guys in the Room: The Amazing Rise and Scandalous Fall of Enron; and, All the Devils Are Here: The Hidden History of the Financial Crisis*

. . . . . .

"*Maeve Rising* is the unflinchingly honest story of Michael, whose anxieties and self-destructive tendencies sabotage every facet of his life: family, friends, career. That is, until Michael discovers her true self as Maeve. This book is important for vividly relating the difficult trans journey toward self-acceptance. But as importantly, it made me appreciate the complexities and difficulties that some of our colleagues bear alone, that could be borne so much more lightly or eliminated if they feel they have the support to show up for work as their authentic selves."

—LLOYD BLANKFEIN, former Chairman and CEO, Goldman Sachs Group, Inc.

· · · · ·

"DuVally shares her life experiences with brutal honesty, sparing no detail about challenges she faced or how she broke down barriers to thrive as the woman she is today. This compelling and personal read will enlighten readers about transgender lives, while reminding all of us that discovering our true selves is a fundamental part of human nature."

—Sarah Kate Ellis, President & CEO, GLAAD (Gay & Lesbian Alliance Against Defamation)

· · · · ·

MAEVE RISING

COMING OUT TRANS
IN CORPORATE AMERICA

MAEVE DUVALLY

Sibylline
PRESS

AN IMPRINT OF ALL THINGS BOOK

Sibylline Press
Copyright © 2023 by Maeve DuVally
All Rights Reserved.

Published in the United States by Sibylline Press,
an imprint of All Things Book LLC, California.
Sibylline Press is dedicated to publishing the brilliant work of
women authors ages 50 and older.
www.sibyllinepress.com

Distributed to the trade by Publishers Group West.
Sibylline Press Paperback
Paperback ISBN: 978-1-7367954-1-5
eBook ISBN: 978-1-960573-01-8
Library of Congress Control Number: 2023935734

Book and Cover Design: Alicia Feltman

MAEVE RISING

COMING OUT TRANS

IN CORPORATE AMERICA

MAEVE DUVALLY

For Jackie, Michi, Myla, Liam, and Connor, who didn't abandon me during my decades of despair, and accepted me when I discovered myself.

PART ONE

EXPERIENCE

"There are as many sorts
of women as there are women."

— Murasaki Shikibu, *Tale of Genji*

AWAKENING

2018

THE VOICE CAME OUT OF NOWHERE.

It was a brisk, late October day and I was sitting in front of my computer in my cramped, unexceptional office on the 29th floor of 200 West Street, Goldman Sachs' headquarters in lower Manhattan.

As I shoveled down my overpriced Goldman cafeteria lunch of wilted lettuce leaves, pasta salad and tasteless tomatoes in my office, a bewildering thought overtook me.

I want to wear makeup tonight.

Scheduled to attend a fund-raising gala at the Marriot Marquis hotel in the heart of Times Square, I had been dreading tripping over the gauntlet of tourists gawking at the tall buildings, not to mention the rude Sesame Street characters trying to make a quick buck. My livelihood depended on my relationships with the top financial journalists in New York at *The New York Times, The Wall Street Journal* and *Bloomberg*, all of whom would be there.

I locked my computer, put on my suit jacket, and headed out of the office. Impetuosity was not in my blood. Caution and deliberation were my watchwords. There was no choice being made. I simply stood up, rushed out of the office, and began to walk.

I knew my destination: Sephora. I had never been inside one before though I had purchased gift certificates online for my daughter.

Goldman Sachs is all the way downtown, right next to the former World Financial Center, where I had worked in two of my previous jobs. The center point of the building complex, now called Brookfield Place, is the Winter Garden, a vast European marbled space punctuated by towering, live palm trees. Built in the 1970s, it usually looked a little bit long in the tooth but today, the palm trees stood proudly, thriving though indoors, and the din that echoed through the confines was redolent with the happiness of its occupants.

Children were joyfully squawking as their nannies, mostly from the Caribbean, chatted noisily with other nannies. Strangely, the world was more in focus, and when I looked closer, it was brighter and lighter than I normally saw it.

Hurrying through, I descended a long escalator, entering the recently built Oculus, a giant, white-ribbed sea creature inhaling and exhaling yet more luxury stores.

Sunlight gushed through the windows on the side and at the top of the structure, which was located on the site of the fallen twin towers. Everything was brilliant white—the marble floor, the bones of the Oculus running up the side and the observation deck. I often walked through on the way to the subway, but it had never been so dazzling.

Had something changed in me?

Lingering in front of the entrance of Sephora, I was awed by the beautiful colors and smells, and suddenly wondered if women knew that, compared to the lives of men, theirs is a world of sensory overload.

Now what do I do?

Finally stepping across the threshold, I was suddenly petrified, but dared not ask anybody for help lest they think the makeup was for me. I locked eyes with one of the young ladies dressed in black who was serving other customers and quickly averted her gaze.

Once I turned my attention to the store's selection, time and the other people didn't seem to exist. It was just me surrounded by makeup. So many different products were calling me to pick them up.

The eye shadow and lipstick were easy, but I was at a loss for the rest. I selected a pink powder I believed to be foundation and a little round mirror in a pink metal case.

Again and again, my hand stretched to pick up something but once I grasped it, it did not feel right, so I put it back. Finally, I had what I thought I needed. At the register, an attractive young black girl with broad orange eye shadow, asked, "Do you have a Sephora frequent shopper's card?"

"Of course not," I wanted to say but simply shook my head and handed over my credit card. When I walked out of the store, I felt exultant.

Skipping back to the office, I noticed I was clutching the black-and-white-striped Sephora shopping bag, which could give me away when I walked back into the Goldman office. I stuffed it under my coat and held my arm against the precious items until I could safely tuck them somewhere in my office, where nobody could see them.

I somehow knew the makeup would make me feel special, but I did not want anybody to know. I applied my makeup so lightly it would barely register in the subconscious of people I met that evening.

And this is what I believed I was doing in the drab gray men's room on the 29th floor as my day ended and I prepared to go to the dinner. I was in a stall looking at the little round mirror. My trove included blue eye shadow, mascara which I smeared on my nose by accident, and the foundation which turned out to be blush.

Sitting on the toilet, I daubed the makeup with one hand and held the small pink mirror with the other. I didn't dare do it in front of the big mirror over the sink. I even paused my task in the stall whenever somebody entered, afraid a sound would escape from me, announcing to all what I was furtively doing.

I had splurged on lipstick, which I applied last. It was Dior—bright red, in a gorgeous black, rectangular case. Savoring every moment, I applied a thick coating of red luxury and wondered how I could have spent my life thus far with naked lips.

I was pleased with how I looked. The fact that I could look at myself in the mirror for more than 15 seconds was miraculous in and of itself. What I saw wasn't perfect, but I liked it just fine.

THE GIRL YOU CAN'T SEEM TO SHAKE

2018

THE DINNER WAS A BLUR. The ballroom was darkened during the speeches and awards presentations so nobody could see me, but I was content, a hot glow emanating from my body. I remember who spoke, but not what they said. Gillian Tett from the *Financial Times* was the MC as she always was. The publisher of the *New York Times* talked about the state and future of journalism, always an in-vogue topic at these dinners.

Sitting next to Lauren, a journalist from *Reuters* whom I also considered a friend, I couldn't restrain myself. I had to tell at least one person.

"I'm wearing some makeup tonight," I whispered perhaps too loudly. A waiter set a glass of wine down and I pushed it away. I'd come to this dinner drunk many times, but I didn't need it anymore.

She had to inch closer to be heard over the speeches and

her eyes swept over my face. "I noticed. It looks good."

Silence. Then she finally asked the obvious, "Why?"

"I just felt like it. I don't really know why. It makes me feel happy," I answered, knowing immediately this sounded evasive, but I didn't have the vocabulary yet to explain it. I picked up my fork, put my head down and poked at the artichokes in my salad.

"Well, you *do* look nice. Let me know if you ever need help buying clothes," she said, starting to laugh. She was renowned for wearing leopard prints.

I pretended to giggle but then paused. *What if this "urge" continued to spiral?*

"Who knows, I may take you up on that," I said jokingly. I grabbed a roll, ripping it in two and plastering it with the whole wheel of butter that was supposed to satisfy half the table.

Then awkward silence.

There was nothing more to say. I had done something bold, and I didn't understand why. The conversation soon devolved into what we usually chatted about: our careers, the quality of the keynote interview, and reporter gossip.

* * *

Yoji yonju gofun. My alarm. A melodic and robotic Japanese women's voice announced it was 4:45 a.m. I had grown attached to this black pyramid-shaped clock and couldn't bear the thought of throwing it away.

Instead of slowly fluttering open, my eyelids shot up as if somebody had yanked them with a hook. High voltage was flowing through me, and I hadn't even sipped a drop of my daily dark roast. I had worn makeup to dinner last night but felt no shame. Maybe I should have been more self-conscious, but the truth was suddenly becoming bigger and more pernicious and perhaps even catastrophic.

I think I want to be a girl.

I had to stop the thought cold. I rolled out of bed, brushed my teeth and put on my Blue Mizuno Wave Riders. The word that flooded my mind was "girl," not "woman" or "female." The thought-stream just felt *young*, not middle-aged as I am in actual time.

I had moved back into the city the previous year from Westchester as my marriage disintegrated and frequently ran to work via Central Park, then down the Hudson River on the west side of the city.

Running was like meditation, allowing me to discard thoughts and focus on my breathing and moving body. Now 57, I started slowly but was warmed up in the ten minutes it took me to get to the park through the still and silent (for now) streets of Manhattan.

Entering the park just north of the Metropolitan Museum of Art, I was relaxed and looked up at Cleopatra's Needle, the Egyptian monolith dating back three dozen centuries. I did this every morning, still in disbelief that this ancient obelisk had ended up in the middle of Central Park.

Sober since January, my life, including my relationships with my soon-to-be ex-wife and my three children, was improving, as was the quality of my work and social life.

I even had friends again.

I'll get rid of that girl *thing*, I mused, but somehow knew I wouldn't. It was as if I was trying to keep the lid on a barrel, but an endless supply of water was bubbling up, making the task impossible.

Sweating, I wiped my forehead with the sleeve of my yellow Boston Marathon running shirt, which I had earned a few years before. The temperature was an ideal low 40s. The park was a bit too crowded for my taste because the New

York Marathon was in a week, and it seemed like all the entrants were getting in their last training runs. I passed the Loeb Boathouse and then the Carousel, both popular tourist destinations on the east side, and was about to turn at the bottom of the park.

I'm fucked. This isn't going away.

I came out of the park at its western base and started walking. Sometimes I just forgot to run when something was really chewing me up on the inside. But, after I crossed Broadway, where traffic was just starting to build for the morning rush, I picked up the pace and headed for the pathway along the river.

This can't be true.

But it was. And, then I couldn't help but wonder—was being a girl something I wanted but didn't consciously know? I just might not be the person I thought I was.

I passed the *Intrepid* aircraft carrier and Chelsea Piers, but I barely noticed them.

Fewer joggers ran along the river in the morning, but the electric bicycles and scooters posed a constant risk. The runners and riders of these conveyances were not very chummy with each other. I usually kept one part of my brain alert to dangers on the path but today I would have been easy pickings for a careless rider. My mind had become a battleground between the old and the new; the known and the unknown; and truth and deceit.

I have wanted to be a girl all my life.

The entirety of my adult life had been spent drinking heavily. Though this embryonic girl idea was new to me consciously, I had already learned that as a sober life took hold, experiences that didn't seem possible might be. As the week wore on, the struggle was tiring me out and I gradually stopped pushing back and tried to focus on work. That didn't mean I fully accepted this new proposition, though.

The fall months at an investment bank are busy. Markets are active, companies are doing deals and the sprint to Thanksgiving and then Christmas is underway. I spent most of my days on the phone talking to reporters or Goldman people acquiring information to give to reporters. I limped into the weekend.

The itch persisted, but I tried my best not to acknowledge or scratch it. If I did, who knows what would happen.

On Sunday night, I went out to dinner with my thirty-year-old daughter Myla. Despite all the slurring, bloodshot eyes, and dazed hangovers she had had to endure through the years, she had sat with me in early sobriety in coffee shops when I was too broken to be able to hold a conversation. I'd just exist there waiting to leave so I could get back into bed and fall asleep to forget the nightmare my life had become.

Our get-togethers were happier now. We ordered our usual: vegetable tempura for me and fermented soybean sushi for her. I pretended everything was normal. That is, I hid behind my work, using it as a front to avoid talking about what was really going on with me.

Ko Sushi is a neighborhood restaurant, and the customers tend to be older, married couples. My daughter is half Japanese, and we usually weren't taken as a parent and daughter. About average in height, Myla had the classic mixed-race issue: To Japanese, she looked very Western, and to Americans, she looked very Asian.

I considered telling her on the spot what had taken root inside of me, but I wasn't quite ready. Besides, the language to match what had been racing through my mind wasn't there yet.

All the men behind the sushi bar and women waiters were Asian but not Japanese. There were lucky white Japanese porcelain cats all over the restaurant and this one evening I couldn't help but break into a smirk and then an audible snicker.

"What's so funny? You usually don't laugh like that," my daughter questioned. She dipped a piece of *natto* roll into the soy sauce and chewed it for about five minutes. Her slow eating annoyed the hell out of me when I was drunk, but not tonight.

"Those cats are so ridiculous, they're cute." I surprised myself by saying this. For a fleeting moment, I felt like a little girl.

Excusing myself to go to the bathroom, I tried the door to the men's room, but it was occupied. The women's room wasn't; I looked over my shoulder and quickly slipped in, bolting the door shut. It was essentially the same as the men's room except there were some fake pink flowers by the sink and it was cleaner. Warm and comforting, it felt different, though.

Sitting upright on the toilet, I was in a place where men weren't meant to be. It was a women's place, and, in that moment, I knew I belonged.

BORN BY THE RIVER LEE

1961

I WAS CONCEIVED ON A PASSENGER SHIP bound from the U.S. to Ireland; and, during the entire passage, my mother experienced a nausea cocktail of seasickness and morning sickness, according to the family folklore. If true, it was an inauspicious start to my life. We berthed in Cork, Ireland, where I was born Michael Stephen DuVally, a name that brought me little joy throughout my life.

My father, Jack, was raised in South Providence, Rhode Island, a working-class enclave of Providence down by the cranes and oil tanks lining the Providence River. My mother, Nancy, grew up in Woonsocket, a decrepit New England town with decaying, boarded-up garment factories once occupied by French Canadians who had flocked to work at the mills during their heyday. After a tour in the military and an undergraduate degree from Providence College, my father somehow ended up in medical school at the University College Cork in southeastern Ireland.

A blond, knock-kneed tot in corduroy overall shorts, I smiled for the camera amid the Cork murkiness while trying to push the lawnmower in the small garden behind our house. My prize possession was a sheepskin rug I curled up upon in front of the fire, willing the heat to warm both me and the rug.

My sister came along two years later and got the cool Irish name I didn't: Deirdre. I was the oldest son and took on all my mother's expectations for success. My father didn't seem to care either way. On her first Christmas, Deirdre was set on my lap for a silly Christmas photo. I got trucks and she, dolls.

We bathed together in our cold drafty house, my mother periodically adding boiling water from a steaming kettle to warm our bathwater. This is when I first noticed the small, soft, hanging string of flesh between my legs. When compared to my sister's clean lines of nothingness, I concluded I had lost the genetic lottery. I watched my penis float in the water after my sister got out and I slumped in the bath to keep my body warm. It was good for peeing, I reasoned, but not for much else.

I vividly recall settling into my father's lap in Flannery's Pub, where he sought refuge every chance he could. Riddled with burn marks and gluey to the touch, the bar was lined with old men drinking dark beer and smoking.

The other men seemed to know my father and called him Doc. One day when he was more animated than usual, he loudly regaled the whole bar about experiences in Ireland—the odd meat he'd eaten, expressions he didn't understand, and customs he had come to adore, like having a roaring fire indoors in the summer. The men reacted boisterously, laughing at his jokes and slapping him on the back. I sat there mutely, mesmerized by my father and the attention he was getting from the other men at the pub. I liked the spirit of the place, a feeling that would stay with me, as I got older.

After that session at Flannery's, we took a stroll in St. Finbarr's Cemetery, where the grass was such a verdant green it hurt the eyes, and the ancient gravestones were speckled with yellow lichen. As my father hoisted me up on his shoulders and sauntered the paths beside the long dead, an ethereal fog crept over the burial grounds, making the gravestones into miniature skyscrapers puncturing the clouds. The twisted limbs on the leafless trees posed for us as we passed them, apparently ready to reposition themselves as soon as we weren't looking.

On these seemingly endless gravel trails, my father sang a plaintive rebel folk song called "The Foggy Dew" and the depressing Irish ditty, "Dan O'Hara," about a man who sells matches for a living and loses pretty much everything of value in his life.

Unable to hold a tune, he moaned the songs in a deep guttural voice. My lids got heavy, and my head started drooping forward. My father didn't notice, lost in the reverie of Murphy's stout and the solitude and comfort of being surrounded by dead people.

He had befriended the Mackey brothers—one who oversaw Flannery's with his wife and the other who owned a couple of butcher shops. Sean the butcher gave us thick plastic bags of chicken livers, our protein for a week. Fried with glimmering slabs of salt pork, they were much appreciated by the family of a struggling medical student. Metallic meat scents rushing through the house meant he had obtained cow liver. He called it steak, but we did not have enough money for such a delicacy, and I already knew steak did not smell like liver frying—nothing did, for that matter. It's no wonder that I'm a vegetarian now.

After dinner one night, my father gently placed two small sacks on the kitchen table, tugged at the drawstrings and unveiled two human skulls.

"They're for studying the body," he explained, dodging my question of where they came from.

"They're two different colors," I observed, keeping the questions coming.

He paused, took a sip of ale, and wiped the excess suds off his mouth. Picking up the dried, brown, fragile skull, he declared, "This is a normal skull."

The effort of putting it down required another long, slow slug of ale.

"This one's Phoebe. She died a painful death from a disease called syphilis," he told me, fascinated by his own explanation.

"Se...fa..." I slowly tried to copy the way he said it.

"Don't worry about spelling it. Just remember the disease killed her." He held the skull up in both hands with reverence, like it was a giant Communion host cradled by a Catholic priest.

"See how big the head is. That's 'cause of the disease." He spoke with a reverence for sickness.

I was seated across the kitchen table from him and had been comfortable until he started talking about illness making the head big. I didn't want that to happen to me. I started to squirm off the chair but my father's eyes, seen through the now empty beer glass, told me to stay.

The skulls had brought a silence with them, and it grew heavier and heavier. I could bear it no more.

"We knew Phoebe, right? That's how you got her skull?"

He put his glass down, walked to the refrigerator, pulled out another bottle of ale and slowly poured it, making sure the foam rose to the top of the glass, but not over. Downing half the glass, he narrowed his eyes and fixed them on me.

"That doesn't matter. I'll tell you why I really have 'em. I keep them to remind myself that we're all going to die."

I couldn't die yet because I almost certainly would go to Hell. My mother constantly called me a bad boy when she scolded me.

The priest at church said as much: Sinners go to Hell where they experience unbearable pain. It was already preordained that I was going there; it was just a question of when.

THE CONFESSIONAL

1966

WITH OUR MOVE TO THE U.S. WHEN I WAS FIVE, a heaviness began to push on me from all directions, making routine parts of life difficult to accept and embrace. By this time, I was the oldest of four, with one more sister, Jennifer, and a brother, John-Peter. We were all two years apart.

I lay half-awake one night thinking about what it would be like if my parents perished in a car crash, and I was left responsible for my siblings. Of course, I could become the savior of the household as an eight-year-old and single-handedly raise the sibling brood. I bathed in reverie. But just as quickly as that came, it was tamped down by a second thought.

I'm no good.

I was a terrible person for wanting the death of my parents in order to become a hero.

We had settled in East Greenwich, Rhode Island, at the base of Narragansett Bay while my father did his residency at Rhode Island Hospital in Providence. Our house was up the hill from the bay, railroad tracks and the heavily trafficked Route 1, Old Post Road.

To counter the terror that frequently arose in me, I threw myself into the Catholic church, which helped for a while. My parents had been raised Catholic. My father abandoned the faith early in life while my mother embraced it. We were parishioners of St. Gregory's, a tan, brick unassuming church nestled in the developments of nearby Warwick. I was not just a Sunday churchgoer but tried to attend every day before school, walking several miles in the dark to be in a place that felt safe. As soon as I could, I became an altar boy and offered to serve at the 6:30 a.m. Mass on weekdays.

Depending on the time of year, as the sun rose, it was sliced into beams by the church's saints in the stained-glass windows. The rays bathed different areas of the church, exposing dust bits which already had been furtively dancing in the air.

The parishioners for the weekday Mass usually consisted of two spinsters who sat together in the front row. Deep in prayer for most of the Mass, they sometimes let their eyes rest on the priest. They ignored me for the most part.

The new church had opened for business the year I was born, and the first pastor was an older man with big jowls and stale cigarette breath—Father Shelley.

"Well done today. I think you're ready for a Sunday Mass and a full church," the priest praised me. The sun was streaming through the back window in the vestry and for a moment shown on both of us.

"I guess so." I wasn't sure. I stepped out of the sun and into the shadow of Father Shelley to protect my eyes.

"What's the matter? You can do anything if you have God's love," he declared confidently and triumphantly. His outstretched arms requested an embrace.

I reluctantly stepped toward him and his fleshy arms, still

covered with vestments, encircled me. The hug was too long, and I began to fidget. "I gotta go to school."

I pulled off my lily-white surplice and started rapidly un-snapping the buttons on my black cassock.

"I'll see you at Mass tomorrow. This is how we save our souls—in service to Jesus." He paused and I thought he might want to hug me again, but I had already hung up my garments and was out the door into the fresh morning air. Hopping my way to school, I felt a lightness to my step, activated by my fresh proximity to God.

First Communion at age seven wasn't particularly meaningful to me but First Confession the next year gave me a chance to do something about sin. My very salvation was at stake. Unknowingly, my father had taught me how the soul and sins interact.

One day with a cigarette in his right hand, he said, "Smoking is such a dirty habit," and added I should never start. I moved away from him and the smoke he had blown all over the house. We were at the kitchen table, his favorite place to teach me all he knew about life.

"I've dissected lungs of smokers. You should see the filth coating them," he said, taking a long drag on his cigarette and washing the smoke down with a Bacardi and coke. "Healthy lungs are big and pink," he said thoughtfully.

How would he know, I thought. He hadn't had lungs like that in years. Mute, I sat on the kitchen chair missing a spindle and, for the first time, understood how a soul works. As sins piled up, the soul became riddled with black stains—mortal sins were deep, grimy blemishes while venial sins were a fainter smear. Confession was the only way to clean the soot away.

The next Saturday, I paused in a pew recalling my sins before slipping into the confessional booth. The priest was in the middle with two stalls for parishioners on each side. I slithered into the right side, waiting my turn. Warm, suffocating and reeking of the breath, sweat and other muck of the hundreds of Catholics who had preceded me here, the booth made me feel faint. A wooden panel near my face slid open, rending my solitude, and presenting a shadowed figure through a screen.

It took me a moment to realize it was Father Shelley, the priest who liked to hug me after Mass. I wasn't supposed to recognize who was on the other side of the screen, but he must have known me by my voice as I knew him. I wondered if it was okay that we knew each other or if it meant that somehow this disqualified me from having my sins forgiven.

I started at once, "Bless me Father for I have sinned—"

A sensation of weightlessness came over me as I relayed my sins. Comforting, this feeling made my time inside the Catholic closet seem worthwhile. But there was a nibble somewhere at the side of my mind.

I am not going to be forgiven by Christ.

I knew the priest and I had hugged him too long. Distracted and annoyed, I grabbed my obnoxious four-year-old brother by the arm as I got into the car after Confession. "Jerk," I muttered.

His cry elicited a scolding from my mother. "And you just got out of Confession!"

I suddenly realized that I was destined to sin frequently and continuously my whole life and Confession was merely a momentary respite from sin. It was so ephemeral as to be almost valueless.

One Sunday, when I was seated in the pews and punching my brother's leg, Father Shelley talked about Jesus coming back to earth some day and taking the pious with him to Heaven. I sat up and listened intently. I wanted to be part of this group. Spending so much time alone, I was already a voracious reader. Now I began devouring fiction and non-fiction about the Rapture, excited by the thought that this chilling, tedious world might be replaced by something where I had a chance to be special. The anticipation was short-lived, as I soon concluded that my intractable sins—teasing my siblings, lying to my parents and even *my hugging* of the priest—had probably already consigned me to Hell.

Attempting to protect myself from this outcome, I prayed fervently before I went to bed, prostrate on my blue and red bedspread with John Paul Jones' cannons blasting and the emblazoned quote, "I have not yet begun to fight."

"Now I lay me down to sleep, I pray the Lord my soul to keep," I prayed, "and if I die before I wake, I pray the Lord my soul to take."

It didn't work. This prayer, on its own, made me an eight-year-old insomniac. One night in the hope of relief, I pushed open the door to my parents' large bedroom, their bed invisible in the darkness.

"Mom, I can't sleep."

Groggy and irritated, my father's voice blared, "Go back to bed *now*."

"What if I can't fall asleep?"

"Just lie in bed and think about whatever makes you happy," my father replied in a still irate, but quieter voice.

I was worried about dying if I fell asleep and he wanted me to think joyful thoughts? *What could he mean? What was joy?* Throwing rocks at trees and trying to walk around in my mother's high-heeled shoes were kind of fun, but did they make me happy? Shoulders slumping, I turned around and left the room. I went straight to my sister Deirdre's bed, crawled in next to her and managed a fitful sleep.

Over time, I became convinced that the inescapable sins

I was saturated with meant I was probably the Devil incarnate. I culled my body for triple sixes, the mark of the beast. When I found no numerals, I had my head shaved just to make sure. Nothing.

Am I evil? I wondered.

No answer ever came back.

* * *

When I was ten, we moved to Rehoboth, Massachusetts, just over the Rhode Island border, after my father got a job in the pathology department of a hospital in Attleboro. With the bigger home came more household responsibilities.

Our backyard was huge and one of my chores was to mow the lawn. As I tried to start the mower, I flooded the carburetor, drawing my father's ire. Unsuccessfully prying open a battery pack with a screwdriver, I drew a headshake saturated in disappointment from my father.

Fishing with him was no better. As I attempted to put a clamworm on a fishhook, I cringed.

"Can't you even bait a hook?" my father growled as he grabbed the pole from me and did it himself. But then it got worse. I caught a fish and now it was my job to twist out the hook from its gasping mouth. My father's disdain for my weakness forced me to yank the hook out even as I detested myself for hurting the poor creature.

I'm no good at anything.

At a middle school dance, a girl named Lisa asked me to dance to "Stairway to Heaven" by Led Zeppelin. I felt real joy. Maybe I would get my first kiss. Then Lisa excused herself to go to the bathroom and never came back. Even when I was on the verge of connecting, something always seemed to go wrong.

Nobody likes me.

By now, I was average height, neither skinny nor fat. My hips stuck out too far, and the blond hair of my youth had turned dirty blonde. My mood soured still further.

In our upstairs bathroom, I pulled up a stool and stared at myself in the mirror, waiting for some sign or inspiration that there was something exceptional about the person looking back at me. Nothing ever happened and I ended up banging my head into the mirror.

I'm very ugly. I hate myself.

My refuge was a Roxbury puddingstone next to our sandy driveway overgrown with weeds. A mishmash of granite and quartz fragments fused with sandstone, the puddingstone was a hard, bumpy mass. The top had been rubbed shiny by constant contact with my butt. I'd spend hours throwing rocks or grinding them down on the puddingstone, chafing off the lime green lichen.

If I was fortunate and my mother had done a big fruit shop, I'd get to play one of my favorite games—swallowing the pits of stone fruits—such as cherries, plums or peaches. The peach stones were not only big but also had spikes growing from either side. The possibility of choking made this contest most alluring.

I'm all alone.

I was full of sin and my path was unclear. I sat on the puddingstone and tempted fate. That seemed like a reasonable way to get through life, right?

PUBERTY

2018

AFTER THE REALIZATION in the Japanese restaurant's bathroom that I was a woman, I embraced it everywhere I went in New York City—except at Goldman Sachs. The stakes were just too high to risk my job at this historically conservative institution. The ten hours a day I spent at work would become interminable if I were not accepted. Now that I was sober, my tolerance for pain had decreased from my drinking days when it had been a constant companion.

The first order of business was choosing a name. Given my Irish heritage and place of birth, I knew I just had to have an Irish name. Scanning the list of Googled "popular Irish girls' names," I eliminated some like "Aoife" and "Oonagh" as too exotic. I considered "Aisling" and "Erin," but once my eyes fell upon "Maeve," I was smitten.

The meaning and origins of the name sealed it for me. Maeve means "she who intoxicates" or "intoxicating beauty," which was, of course, a perfect foil for he (Michael) who was intoxicated for most of his life. An actual or mythological warrior, Queen Maeve was strong-willed and best known for stealing Ulster's prize bull stud in the Irish epic, *The Cattle Raid of Cooley.*

My last decision was whether to use the Gaelic spelling, Meabh, or the anglicized spelling. On the one hand, the pronunciation was basically the same, but the Gaelic spelling would surely stump Americans and that was too much if being transgender was layered in. Choosing a name had been a thoroughly unique and enjoyable part of being trans that most cisgender people never get to experience. But just because I selected a name, I still didn't know if it suited me. It's like naming a dog and calling it for the first time. The dog is usually confused for a bit.

Fortunately, there is one ubiquitous place to experiment: Starbucks.

Though I was reasonably confident nobody would figure out what I was doing, I was nervous as I walked into the Starbucks on Second Avenue between 74th and 75th Street. It was a typical Starbucks, chaos in the customer line and chaos behind the counter. I could barely hear anything and was sure I'd have to repeat my order because the cashier never seemed to be listening.

Stepping up to the counter, I ordered. "Venti Cappuccino please."

The attendant countered, "Name, please."

I looked down at the ground. It was harder to say my name the first time than I thought it would be. Finally, I declared, "Maeve," and repeated it for good measure.

Just my luck, the young cashier was androgynous with a coating of tattoos and a littering of piercing punctures. They had trouble with the spelling, so I jumped in to help, clearly uttering, "M A E V E," and then before I knew what I was doing, added, "It rhymes with brave."

Now I waited, glancing furtively at the other New Yorkers around me, wondering if anybody would notice that somebody who looked like a man was picking up a drink meant for Maeve.

My heart literally fluttered when my drink was ready and the barista called, "Venti Cappuccino for Maeve."

"Thank you so much," I exclaimed, fishing a five-dollar bill out of my pocket and stuffing it in the tip jar.

* * *

Alcoholics Anonymous was my first "out" refuge. From the time I moved back into a Manhattan sober house in the summer of 2017, I attended AA meetings on the Upper East Side. Around Halloween, I went to a meeting I regularly attended on Wednesdays wearing makeup for the first time and the most gender-neutral clothes I could find in my wardrobe. Somebody made a crack about me wearing makeup for Halloween and I smiled uncomfortably. The room was typical AA, a large cafeteria in a religious school. The floors were polished daily and harshly reflected the fluorescent lights, drawing squints when we walked in from the dark.

When it came time for me to share, I remember my face turning red as I recapped my recovery over the last nine months.

"I drank off and on for nearly four decades," I began. "I now realize I was a prisoner in a dark room, all alone and terrified. And, once I started working the program of Alcoholics Anonymous, the urge to drink not only disappeared, but my life got better."

Pausing and taking a deep breath, my lips began to quiver, and I said out loud for the first time in my life, "Tonight, I can tell you, in this safe space, that I am transgender and have wanted to be a girl all my life. Nobody is more surprised by this than me." The experience was eerily similar to saying I was an alcoholic for the first time.

Then, I added, "Please call me Maeve, in honor of my Irish heritage, from now on. Thank you."

All my blood had risen to my head, dizzying and threatening to topple me. I did not cry because I could not cry yet. But it was another threshold crossed.

After the meeting, a young woman named Liz whom I'd never met came up to me and said, "That was so special to hear you come out and I don't even know you."

We became fast friends and AA buddies thereafter.

* * *

Though I did not know it at the time, the next seven months would become an extended rehearsal for my next act: coming out at Goldman Sachs. But I was too busy going through puberty for the second time as a fifty-six-year-old. I found a therapist specializing in transgender patients and made my first visit to the Mount Sinai Center for Transgender Medicine and Surgery. Then I set about further remaking my appearance.

My first excursion to buy clothes was to The Loft, a block away from my apartment. Just as I had at Sephora, I hesitated at the threshold, but then stepped into the brightly lit store, determined to buy some clothing. It being late fall, I purchased long lime-green and pink sweaters, pink corduroy pants and a pair of tight jeans. I kept waiting for the gender police to arrive and lock me up, but I simply walked up to the register and paid.

For some reason, I had deliberately avoided wearing anything pink my entire life, but I could not get enough of the color now. Eventually, I'd have pink nails, pink jackets, pink boots, and pink dresses.

I also made a stop at Victoria's Secret, which was a few doors down in the Oculus from Sephora. It was at the end of a long corridor of stores so I could see the alluringly darkened room and brightly colored bras and other lingerie as I approached.

Without warning, I got an erection, which lasted a while, forcing me to take off my jacket and hold it over my midsection. I ended up buying several bras, but the excursion was sullied by my arousal. I felt I spoiled what should have been thoroughly feminine experience by having a quintessential male stimulation. Fortunately, I had already made a trans friend in AA, and she assured me that this was not an uncommon experience. I was learning it's sometimes hard to disentangle sex and gender, particularly for a trans person.

With clothes and makeup out of the way, it was time to think about my hair. Since the night with Myla when I accepted the fact that I was transgender, I had been reading online for options on appearance. Next to having a penis and thick white and black body hair on my shoulders, chest and back, what I hated most about my appearance was my receding hairline. The lack of head hair was just one more reason never to look in a mirror.

From what I could tell, I wasn't a great candidate for surgical hair restoration, so wigs were the only option. After some more digging, I found myself walking into Hanna Wigs, located in Midtown East. The store was one small room plastered in mirrors with various wigs on models' busts. Each head's features such as eyes, mouth, eye shadow and any other touches of makeup were painted on, creating the impression for customers of being surrounded by dozens of creepy doll heads ready to become animated and attack.

There was a glass counter with more wigs on it, behind which sat two Asian saleswomen. The wigs in this shop were mostly synthetic and the price point was reasonable as wigs go—a couple of hundred dollars.

By now, I had perfected the art of buying something feminine without asking anybody for help. I circled the wig showroom twice; smiling each time I passed the counter where the wig ladies were sitting. They observed me warily and correctly decided that they were going to have to initiate the conversation.

The younger one with long hair (it looked real), gently inquired, "Is there something specific you are looking for?"

Wigs seemed different to me than makeup or clothes and required a higher level of transparency with the shopkeepers.

"I'm transgender and am looking for a wig," I said, avoiding her gaze.

"We have many transgender customers," she said. "We show them much respect."

I failed to respond and must have looked skeptical. Glancing over at the entrance, I could be out on the street in ten seconds and this discomfort would all be over, I thought. Mustering a totally fake smile, I looked back at the shop person who had been talking to me.

"Oh, we'll make you look pretty," she retorted. I figured she said that to every customer, but I liked the sound of it. I relaxed.

She handed me a nylon mesh cap to cover my hair, which I couldn't get on. One side always slid up when I tried to put the other side on. Then she handed me a dirty blonde wig with shoulder length hair. Of course, I did not know it at the time, but it was bob style a la Anna Wintour.

The longhaired attendant adjusted it just right on my head. It was heavy and made my head start sweating right away.

"It's beautiful on you," the other person, who had been mute up until now, suddenly chimed in.

My first impression was positive, but it was such a radical departure from the look of the me I knew, I needed time to process it. Fortunately, no other customers had entered the store: I probably would have bolted.

Mesmerized and terrified I would be judged harshly in the outside world, I sat silently and still for ten minutes. Emptying my mind of every thought, I just stared and stared, which was still a new and disorienting experience for me,

Finally, I swallowed my fear and said, "I'll take it." I searched my thoughts to see if there was any pushback. Nothing.

She explained how to wash it and took my charge card.

"Shall I put it in a bag?" she asked, holding out a plain gray plastic shopping bag for me to put it in.

I shook my head, thanked the two ladies and walked out into the feeble late afternoon sun.

I watched "my hair" bending backwards with the wind, which awed and titillated me. I had never really had long hair in my life and certainly not recently.

Over time, I graduated to more expensive, human hair wigs and then a system, which integrated my own grown-out hair with a hairpiece sewn in, but I had crossed another verge at Hanna Wigs.

I had intended to wear the wig outside for just five minutes and then stuff it away. Placing my bags on a nearby wall, I raised my hands to take it off, but I wanted to see it one more time, so I took out the little pink mirror.

I couldn't bear the thought of taking it off just yet. "Fuck it. Wear it home on the subway," I ordered myself.

So I did.

FIREBIRD SUITE

2018

HAVING NOT SEEN MY DAUGHTER since the night at Ko Sushi, I summoned her a couple of weeks later to Café Bleriot XI on East 85th Street. A small eclectic coffee shop with a European flair, it was tucked away on a side street, unlike Starbucks, which was always conspicuous on one of the main avenues.

The walls, which loomed over the two small tables that took up almost the entire customer space, were covered in greenish-brown wallpaper decorated with fleur-de-lis. Life had come full circle: Myla and I used to meet here when I first got sober. I hoped the conversation today would be better than the ones I had with her back then when even the effort to produce words overwhelmed me.

Arriving a few minutes early, I sat down and looked at myself in my small pink mirror. The current me was wearing a wig, tight jeans, a beige sweater that I'd bought at the fashion label Theory, and my makeup, which thankfully, I had become more skillful at applying. Nodding slightly, I put the mirror away.

Myla walked in, her eyes narrowing for a fraction of a second. If I weren't her parent, I wouldn't have even noticed.

"A lot of change in the world these days," I said, opening the conversation. My children both enjoyed and mocked my attempts at humor.

"Change can be a good thing," she retorted, not skipping a beat.

I ordered our coffees and a scone for Myla.

"I guess the cat was out of the bag as soon as you saw me." Not knowing what to say next, I was relieved when the shop-keeper announced our coffees were ready. The time it took to fetch them allowed me to re-gather my poise.

"I'm transgender," I announced. I watched the crumbs tumble from her scone as she took her first bite. For some rea-son, there were a lot of moments recently when time seemed to slip to a different, slower loop.

We discussed my initial realization and how long I'd known. Then, she fixed a stare on me and asked, "Can I still call you Dad?"

Admonishing myself for not having thought of that in advance, I just let the answer spill out of my mouth. "Of course, you can." If I had refused, she would have gone along, but I had put those close to me through so much. In the scheme of things, whether I was called "Mom" or "Dad" by my children did not rank very high.

The conversation then turned to my clothing. I asked her where she liked to shop these days, something I'd only done in the past around Christmas when I wanted to get her a gift card. She said she liked Zara, an affordable clothing retailer popular with younger women.

Though I struggled to form the request, I found myself ask-ing her whether she wanted to go clothes shopping with me.

Several days later, we met in front of Zara in Midtown,

right across from Bloomingdale's. Most of the shoppers were in their twenties and the clothes styles naturally were tailored to that demographic. I'd already decided there was not much for me to buy there but I did not want to leave empty handed.

"I see some things I like," I said, putting pressure on myself to buy. The two floors were cavernous and as opposed to typical New York stores, there was ample room to browse without shoppers jostling me with their overstuffed bags.

"I'm just happy that you see something you want to buy," she said. Myla is non-materialistic, an idealist and socialist. I insisted she purchase something, but I doubted she would.

The fake fur coats caught my eye, and I hurried over. There were pink, dark blue and white coats. We ran our fingers over the soft outer fake fur. I looked at the price, a couple of hundred dollars. I would need to get some staid work coats, but this could be my fun one.

After gathering up one in my size, I went on to buy some tight black felt pants and a loose-fitting, striped, long-sleeved shirt.

Myla just contentedly watched, and I gave up urging her to buy something. Outside, I couldn't help myself saying one more time, "I would have paid if you wanted to buy something, you know." I pleaded, hoping she'd go back in.

"It's fine. I have enough." She could be warm but also distant at times. I was an expert at being distant and it was easy for me to recognize it in other people.

She earned her living teaching and performing classical piano, which gave her a great degree of freedom but not financial comfort in a place like New York. Since she'd been a student, I had been slipping her money whenever we met, and I always did it in the same way.

I opened my purse and fished out a hundred-dollar bill, holding it halfway between us. "I suppose you don't want this then?" I teased.

We both smiled. "I'll always take money."

It passed between us. We hugged and then parted; the gulf that sometimes existed between us diminished, as it always was whenever we were together.

AUTOPSIES

1975

THE SOMBER CHILDHOOD DINNERS we had in Rehoboth were always eaten as a family. My father, having just arrived from work, was stone cold sober and not very happy about it. He complained about drafts in the kitchen and raged about somebody stealing the butter that was only meant for him. The four of us children shoveled our food in to be done as quickly as possible.

Toward the end of the meal as he finished his second glass of wine or beer, my father became more relaxed and pleasant. From experience, we knew that drinks number three and four right after dinner were the sweet spot.

Dinner fare was equally unpleasant. My parents never quite abandoned the cheapness they were forced into during their years in Ireland and frequently tried to serve us guts—heart, liver, and kidneys. We would have to sit there and finish the guts no matter what. And then there was the matter of the farm animals we raised and grew attached to. They could very easily wind up cooked and on a plate before us, with my parents lying about their origin.

My mother held the house together, just as she, as the oldest female child in her family, had to hold together her household headed by her alcoholic father. She did her best, chauffeuring us to sports games, helping with homework, cooking, cleaning and caring for us when we were sick. But it was as if she was the nanny of the household, and she was under no obligation to show regular care and concern for the children. And, when she did, it was overblown and hysterical, which often sent my siblings and me to my father when we had a problem; he'd be calm and philosophical about situations when we caught him drunk.

My father provided a comfortable life for us, but he was a very sad and sick man. My sister had a pet rabbit we simply called "the chinchilla" for its breed. A curious and playful rabbit, the chinchilla hopped around and curled up in Deirdre's lap when we brought her into the house to watch TV with us.

One of us always asked my mother or father what the meat for dinner was.

On this night, my mother answered, "chicken."

"I love chicken," my father said a bit too energetically.

Browner, less fatty, and chewier than chicken, the meat immediately raised doubts in my mind. I caught Deirdre's eye, and she was clearly concerned. We couldn't leave the table yet but when we could, Deirdre and I ran down the driveway to the rabbit hutches. The chinchilla's cage was empty.

Besides slaughtering pets, serving them to us for dinner and forcing us to eat guts, Dad delighted in sharing details with us of the autopsies he had performed, even at the dinner table.

Pathology, his specialty, is perhaps the best area of medicine for a misanthrope. There is no way he could have delivered devastating news to a grieving young couple in a compassionate manner. Pathology was perfect for him. He basically sat in front of a microscope all day and looked at biopsies, deciding for example, if something was cancerous or non-cancerous. Extrapolating from my later days as an active drunk, I can only imagine him being fidgety early in the day when he was still in the throes of a hangover. The few times he had to drop me off somewhere on the way to work, I knew not to say anything for fear he might erupt angrily.

To the extent he was capable of exhibiting affection, he dribbled it on my sister Deirdre, bringing her into work on Sundays when nobody else was in and he had to do an autopsy. She helped him haul bodies out of the freezer.

Perhaps I should not have considered it bizarre that he developed a passion for dissecting dead family pets. We had a lovely Great Dane named Venus who had the typical short, big-dog life; she died in the fall one year. My father threw the dog's carcass in the shed he had built by a pond and let it freeze solid. Throughout December, my siblings and I would sneak into the shed and peak under the giant tarp where Venus lay motionless.

Suddenly, one day in the dead of winter, he fired up a big industrial space heater to thaw out the frozen interior, set up an autopsy table and meticulously took the dog apart. I'll never forget walking into the shed where I saw Venus, now cut open on the table. I ran out into the woods as quickly as I could. I really don't know what killed the dog, but I'm not at all sure that was the point for my father anyway.

For me, the one I will never forget was coming down to the basement to get some food out of the pantry. My father had an ever-present cigarette in his mouth, and by his side, his green plastic quart cup, which was a third ice, a third Bacardi white rum, and a third caffeine-free Diet Coke. He hadn't noticed me as he bent over, intensely moving a hacksaw through the head of a just-deceased family cat whose lower body was held tightly by his vise. My father generally was not a happy man, but he was smiling.

What I most remember about that house in Rehoboth was being all alone in the attic as a ten-year-old, freezing. Tree shadows waved in the moonlight just outside my window. The wind pounded on the thin glass, threatening to break into my already frigid room. In the dead of winter, I pictured everybody warm below and me occupying the only polar space in the house because my mother would not allow me to use the expensive electric heat. I lay on my right side facing away from the window and on the edge of the bed so if I tilted one inch further rightward, I would fall off onto the tundra of the floor. I wanted the night to end. The days were not great, but they were better.

Sometimes I'd slip downstairs and crawl into bed with my sister. Her room was warm and had comforting girl smells like lavender body cream and minty shampoo.

My father had an antique gold-plated microscope that he kept in the attic. I found it one day along with a box of slides and brought it into his study. They were frosted white on one end and had samples smushed by a top covering. I put the slide under the bottom of the viewing tube and looked intently. I was shocked to see what I could only imagine were the long, moving legs of something akin to a daddy long legs spider. I looked down at the slide and then there was nothing there moving. I looked again and they were back. I pulled my father over.

"Dad, you've got to see this—there's some kind of spider or something like that," I shouted. This felt like a special occasion because I was using his microscope in his study, a place we generally were not allowed.

He was annoyed that I'd taken him out of his alcoholic reverie, but he removed his glasses and looked.

"There is nothing there except the blood smear on the slide," he said in a monotone.

"I swear there is," I said defending myself. I described the creature as having about a dozen legs like a spider, though all I could see were the legs.

He paused a minute, considering his words which he usually did not.

"Sometimes I think you're plain stupid," he uttered. Then he crushed me, adding, "Those are your eyelashes magnified through the microscope."

How was I supposed to know?

"If all this bothers you a lot, just stop using the damn microscope and put it back where it belongs, in the attic," he declared, turned, and went back downstairs.

My answer to my father's cruelty and neglect was to become as diligent in my studies as possible. After dinner, I retired to my room to read and study for hours.

But I always fell into the same trap. There was inevitably something I heard at school, or I had read in the newspaper about the state of the world that I wanted to ask about.

Muteness was the safest strategy: Comments provoked tangents upon tangents upon tangents. If I started posing questions, I'd be trapped. He'd smoke cigarette after cigarette and continually freshen up his cocktail with more Bacardi white.

"That idiot peanut farmer is ruining our country," he started ranting one night about our newish president Jimmy Carter. "All he wants to do is steal my money and take away my guns."

The next phrase was a foregone conclusion. "They can have my gun when they pry my cold, dead fingers from around it," he tried to say proudly, but he was slurring by then.

I nodded. He continued with his life lessons.

"What do I always say: Trust no one," he said, raising his voice as if to emphasize the importance of this wisdom.

Feebly protesting, I whispered, "So that means I shouldn't trust you or anybody in the house?"

"We're your family," he replied, but immediately added, "But we'll screw you in the end."

That was my cue to escape and head back up to my room. After reading for a half hour, I came down for a glass of water to see him on his knees and shins in front of the fireplace, flicking ashes from his cigarette in the direction of the fireplace but not even getting close. His drink sat next to him on the carpet, ready to be spilled. It didn't really matter because that carpet was soaked with years of dog and cat urine. He was not bald but, when he drank, the long black and white strands of his combover fell all around his face and his eyes would open and shut. I swore I would never be like him.

He boasted about being on a submarine during the Korean War, but we had no idea what that type of life was like. For that matter, we knew virtually nothing about him except the most basic facts.

"What was it like being on a submarine?" I inquired once and only once.

He looked at me coldly. "It was hot and cramped," he replied. I wasn't sure whether he was deliberately trying to make the conversation difficult.

"Did you ever kill anybody in battle?" I offered, hopeful this might entice him to respond to a question I was honestly curious about.

He took another swig of his drink and lit another cigarette. "That's not something a father talks about with his son."

Some years later, he resigned in shame from the one pathology job he had had for most of his adult life. We didn't really know what was going on at the time because my family never talked about anything. I just knew my father was more taciturn than usual and even the evening drink did not enliven him.

His whole life was the hospital, where he felt like royalty around the nurses. Without it, the miserable man just became more miserable.

THE MOSQUITO THAT ENDED A RELATIONSHIP

1981

THE ORANGE ASIAN FIREBALL illuminated the early morning sky, obliterating the smog and thin clouds. The sun seemed so menacing it could disintegrate the cranes lining the harbor with its focused rays. I was not in Providence, Rehoboth, or Cork anymore.

I had arrived in Tokyo the night before and was getting my first peek at the country in daylight. Woozy with jetlag and a medium hangover, I tried to recall my first impressions of Japan, but my memory was fuzzy and damaged from emptying my duty-free bottle of Johnnie Walker Black on the flight over.

After the terror of my adolescent years, I had gotten on with my life, making accommodation with my internal recriminations: They were still there but weren't new anymore. Solitude still was the most comfortable, but I had developed ways to be alone that would not alarm those around me.

As a teenager, I took refuge in a basketball hoop put up along with floodlights illuminating our driveway. Playing for hours after school each night, I felt the skin on my hands split in the winter from the constant contact with the ice-laden ball.

Reading was my passion and Nietzsche, Dostoevsky, Kurt Vonnegut, Raymond Chandler, and Marcus Aurelias were the friends I never had at school. Our teachers made us read mostly men, but I discovered *Orlando: A Biography,* by Virginia Woolf and borrowed it again and again from the library. It was such a queer story—a male poet who changes into a woman and lives for a long time.

I studied incessantly, at one point attempting to *memorize* the dictionary so I could get an 800 on my SATs. I was named "Most Studious" my senior year, an honor to me, but probably dweeby to everybody else. I had a handful of friends I met periodically—just enough to not be branded a loner.

Following my father to Providence College, I became a binge drinker Thursday to Sunday, joining the few friends I had at the Providence Marriott Hotel's happy hour, all-you-can-drink for ten bucks. At the pace I drank, I was happy only for a short time.

After two years there, life was barely working for me so I moved just about as far from the east coast of the United States as I could—Japan.

I'd never flown anywhere farther than Los Angeles but here I was in August 1981 disembarking from the plane in Anchorage for a refueling stop before beginning the second eight-hour leg of my journey. Stuffed Arctic creatures adorned the walls of the airport and unique smells from all kinds of Asian restaurants—udon and sushi shops and Chinese stir fry—circulated in the cozy airport with looming snow-capped mountains in the distance. Anchorage was by far the most exotic place I had been to in my life, but it would be eclipsed.

My journey ended in Hirakata City, a bedroom community halfway between Osaka and Kyoto and home of Kansai

Gaidai, which had an exchange student swap arrangement with Providence College. For my first semester, I had also opted to live with a homestay family. All I knew beforehand was it consisted of a married couple with two boys.

My first week, I met Atchan, an energetic sophomore woman who was going to be an exchange student at Providence College the next year. I had the most innocent of intentions and thought I would just offer to answer her questions about the U.S. It all felt safe to me. Her mother taught English and had hosted homestay students, so Atchan spoke impeccable, unaccented English.

"How's Japan?" she asked breezily. We were hanging out in the main Kansai Gaidai campus courtyard. The space was too small for so many students and had a shoddy, trampled look. The grounds were either dirt or concrete, littered with cigarette butts and empty canned coffee containers spilling from overstuffed trash receptacles.

Just then something fell out of her mouth onto her lap. "How embarrassing," she said, holding up a fake front tooth. She took out a small mirror and carefully placed it back on its artificial stand in the top of her gums. We grew quiet; her out of embarrassment, and me in astonishment. I looked at the ground and a condom, which hadn't made it into the trash can and was still seeping its contents onto the earth.

Atchan suddenly started laughing and I joined in.

"Let's not let a tooth destroy a good conversation," I said, breaking the ice. Groups of students in twos, threes and fours passed us. The population was homogenous, but I was used to that. Minorities were just that in Rehoboth.

"I like Japan very much," I said in the local tongue, but she ignored my still pidgin Japanese and responded in English.

"I'm glad to hear that. Where are you living?" she questioned. A formation of male students came jogging by in karate outfits and bare feet chanting something guttural and warlike.

"Katano, at the end of that line from Hirakata. I've been running up the mountains and found a cool shrine in the woods I like to visit." I was boasting a little.

"I'd rather be surfing," she retorted.

"You surf?" I asked, glancing at my watch. I was going to be late for my Japanese history class, but I didn't care.

"Well, my boyfriend does, at Enoshima Island."

I felt defeated. I was already starting to like her. My crushes always began quickly and crashed soon after. Rubbing salt into my wounded affection, a couple on the bench next to us was kissing passionately and making loud grunting noises.

Atchan stood up. "Nice meeting you. Hope we talk again; I'm off to class." Before turning her back, she stuck her finger in her mouth one more time and pushed on the misbehaving tooth. She smiled again and was gone.

* * *

I had girlfriends for short periods in high school, but the relationships never lasted very long because I sabotaged them.

Joanna and I had been going strong for about two months during my senior year. This one just might work, I thought but my hope soon evaporated in an instant.

We were outside in the school parking lot talking on a glorious spring day when the sun was just beginning to exert some strength after a long New England winter.

She hadn't realized a mosquito had landed on her right cheek and for some reason paralysis prevented me from telling her. The rest of the bug experience must have lasted several seconds at most, but it played out in super slow motion.

"Don't you love Mr. Day's English class on *Macbeth* when he yells out 'self-aggrandizement'?" she said, laughing.

"I really liked that, too." I had to say something, but I was mesmerized by the mosquito. It stamped its six legs up and down several times to make sure it had good leverage. It then paused in anticipation and viciously plunged its proboscis into her face. I imagined the first taste of blood must be like heroin euphoria for a junkie.

"What are you doing during your free period? Do you want to study together in the auditorium?" I didn't hear her.

By now, the mosquito must be getting lightheaded. Though it had only fed for a second its engorged abdomen already glowed red.

Joanna blinked. She realized the mosquito was on her face and she brought her right hand up from her side and smashed it, spotting her face with little squirts of blood—her blood that the mosquito had made its own.

"Ew. Why didn't you tell me? Didn't you see it?" she asked accusingly as she pulled a tissue out of her bag and wiped the blood off.

"I didn't. I was too busy concentrating on our conversation," I lied. I had to get away from her immediately. My fascination with the unfolding drama on her face had suddenly and inexplicably turned to revulsion and it was overpowering. She shrugged and we went off to our next classes. I broke up with her the next day, saying that my feelings weren't quite right, and I wasn't ready for a relationship.

She seemed to sense in a general way what was plaguing me. "Sometimes at the start of the relationship when you have confusing, mixed-up feelings you have to sit in those and plow through," she said, making one last attempt to save the relationship.

Wise words, but how could I admit the disgust I now felt for her, all because I had witnessed a mosquito traipse across her face and feed?

FROM NAMBATO HIROSHIMA

1982

IT WAS THERE IN HIRAKATA that I felt liked for the first time in a long time. In the early 1980s, except for certain parts of Tokyo and Osaka, Westerners were not common in Japan. Although the Japanese value their civilization and history, they have a natural attraction to Western culture and the Western aesthetic. Being a young white American, I was welcomed. Because nobody needed to know me as an individual, nobody could reject me personally. It was so perfect for me that I could not have drawn up a better script.

After two months in Japan, I felt different. Identity is like that. The external circumstances had conspired to change my perception of myself for the better. I met girls—lots of girls, though my carnal baptism was inauspicious. *Had I forgotten how I felt about my penis when I viewed it in the tub years ago?*

All the male exchange students around me were apparently having sex with frequency. A part of me didn't want to participate in this game but I had been left out for so much of my life, I eventually jumped in, though reluctantly.

Accompanied by my fellow exchange students, a New Mexican hippy named Mark and a half-Japanese ruffian from Australia named Andrew, we were soon prowling the discos in Osaka patronized by foreigners and Japanese girls attracted to foreigners. The tunes were from the early Eighties. "Let's Groove Tonight" by Earth Wind and Fire and "Your Kiss is on My List" by Hall and Oates played endlessly.

"You're a virgin?" Mark both questioned and declared indignantly between classes. Incredibly bright with a scruffy beard and thick glasses, he'd been offered scholarships to Ivy League schools, but he had opted for a less taxing college in his home state, so he'd have plenty of time to get high, play the guitar and chase girls.

We were hanging out by the Yodo River, concrete on all sides like most rivers in metropolitan Japan, with our shirts off, something you probably wouldn't see the Japanese doing. One night several months later, I threw all my clothes, piece by piece, into this stream after getting out of a taxi with a lapful of vomit.

I nodded in shame at Mark's question and watched a white rice cooker bobbing in the flowing water. But he smiled and wagged a finger at me. "No friend of mine stays a virgin, especially here."

I'd been staring at the ground but looked up at him. The idea of sex petrified me.

Was it because I hated myself and feared rejection? Or was it because I didn't like the body I was in?

"I know this one disco in Osaka where they let in *gaijin* for free," Hasegawa chimed in, using the Japanese word for foreigner, "outsider," as we all did. "And we can get booze for free" he added, bouncing in his spot with excitement.

"Hell yeah. That's the one," Mark chimed in.

The river was pristine for the moment—no garbage floated on the top but who knew how many bicycles lurked underneath. Then a pink stuffed cat, waterlogged and dead, caught my eye. I shivered. If this went much further, I'd have to go with them.

"You guys go scout out this *gaijin* disco. If it's as good as you've heard, then I'll be there next weekend. I'm behind— tests next week," I exclaimed, holding my breath, and hoping this would work.

"Not going to happen. We need to get you into the win column," Mark said, flicking the end of his Mild Seven butt into the river.

I capitulated, not liking disagreement. "You win." I want- ed to get out of this conversation and go to a dive bar, Sake Dojo, just up the road where they dumped leftover miso soup and beer dregs on the floor. They also offered a free dozen pork dumplings if you ate (and kept down) three dozen.

"No, you'll win." Andrew said. He pointed toward the Yodo. "I guarantee you success or I'll take a swim in that."

That night, we were on the train to Osaka drinking tall- boy cans of Kirin beer we bought from a vending machine, whooping it up until we got to Namba. We walked along the Dotonbori River, bordered by such a garish outburst of green, red, and blue neon, it might as well have been day.

We walked into Jimmy's, the special disco Andrew said cod- dled foreigners. It was, of course, dark, with a bar area adorned in mirrors. There were red-and-yellow colored squares on the floor and walls, all giving off a muted light. In the back was the actual dance floor, which now was ringed by young girls danc- ing alone and staring at themselves in the mirrors.

Mark went over to a couple of girls, picked one for himself and forced me to introduce myself to a girl named Mamiko, which means auspicious child, and she certainly was for me. Nothing happened for a couple of weekends, but we were soon in the Namba-Rent-A-Room, which charged by the hour, 4,000 yen for 60 minutes.

The room was small with a twin bed and nightstand. The theme from *Romeo and Juliet* was playing in a continuous loop. It was so sappy and annoying. Other than its spareness, the only indications of what the room was intended for were the red sheets and crimson heart-shaped pillows. We undressed quickly and were immediately cold, so we hurried under the covers for warmth. Mamiko slid the condom over me as I watched in fascination.

Rolling on top of her, I entered her but once there, I froze. *Now what do I do?*

I never received the guide that told me I was supposed to move back and forth to create feeling on the penis. Not only was I a virgin, but I'd never masturbated, discussed sex, or looked at a *Playboy Magazine*. I panicked. *Why had everybody else gotten the playbook for sex while I didn't? It just wasn't fair.*

Turning my attention away from myself and back to the situation at hand, I was tempted to bail out literally, put on my clothes and rush out of the Namba-Rent-A-Room as fast as I could. I imagined lying to Andrew and Mark because they were certainly going to ask me for details when I saw them later tonight. My terror got worse, and I began to lose my erection, which induced still more horror.

Fortunately, Mamiko was patient and grabbed my ribcage with both hands, literally pushing me back and forth. After that, instinct finally kicked in, and I relaxed a little. Though I had drunk seven or eight whisky and Cokes, I was suddenly stone cold sober, which was a place I didn't want to be.

The accursed *Romeo and Juliet* song continued to blare. I started counting pubic hairs on the floor by the bed. But then something unexpected happened. I suddenly felt full down there—so full that I burst.

I was both exultant at finally having experienced a male rite of passage and disgusted with having discovered the other way a penis is used. Tearing the condom off, I tossed it into the trash and quickly slipped my underwear back on.

Mamiko must have been confused. My bifurcated self would giddily kiss her only to pull away and slip into morbid preoccupation. We dressed quietly and efficiently, after which I ushered her out of the room. Pausing, I took one last look at room number 32 in the Namba-Rent-A-Room.

Why is nothing ever easy for me? I brooded.

We kissed economically and antiseptically by the Dotonbori River, teeming with couples perhaps on their way to their own Namba-Rent-A-Rooms. We exchanged phone numbers and promised to meet again soon, though I knew I wouldn't see her for at least a while. There was much to process. I kept notifying myself that life was getting good. Maybe if my reports to myself were frequent and convincing enough, I would believe them.

* * *

For the second semester, I moved into my own apartment with a student named Kelly, who had a taste for tuna fish but due to being unable to read Japanese, ate cat food most of the semester. The dump we rented had no shower, no bath, no flush toilet, and no heat, but it was very, very cheap. I nearly burnt it down several times after I came home from the discos drunk, flipped on a space heater and fell asleep. I'd wake up to smoke and gentle flames threatening to lick my face as my *futon* caught fire.

Toward the end of the semester, my homestay mother offered to take me and her two sons down to where she was raised, Hiroshima, to see the Peace Memorial Museum and meet her family. We spent a somber day walking around the museum and learning about the atomic bomb from the perspective of the victims. After a feast and a lot of beer, I crawled into my freshly made *futon* bed, savored the crisp, clean sheets and prepared to doze off for the evening.

The *fusuma* paper door to my room opened with a precision wooden slide and my homestay mother entered.

I had been staying over at the homestay family's house one night a week during the second semester. I enjoyed a home-cooked Japanese dinner and taught the boys English before going to sleep in my bedroom from the first semester. About once a month, my homestay mom came into my room (of course, while her husband was away) and lay next to me. And, so, she was at it one last time.

That night, she was wearing a white nightgown with blue trim that glowed in the moonlight. She was neither attractive nor unattractive—she was a typical Japanese housewife wandering about the house with an apron on most of the day. Tonight, her eyes were fully open, and pupils dilated. In the past, I had looked into her eyes, trying to figure out why she was in my bed. I had always turned away and she would silently slip out.

That night, I did not turn away. I kept looking into her eyes. *Fuck it.*

I moved closer. Her shallow breathing became deeper, and she closed her eyes. I kissed her but instead of warm and wet lips, they were dry and flaky, but it didn't matter. There was no turning back now.

I reached up the nightgown. She was panty-less and wet already. She suddenly yanked off the nightgown and pulled me on top of her and we copulated, which is exactly the right word for the mechanical act performed. I came quickly, which is what I think she wanted and rolled off. She went to the dresser, came back with a box of tissues, and dabbed at the wetness between her legs and then the wetness on my penis.

She put her nightgown back on, turned her back and was gone. No word had been uttered between us, nor would we ever talk again except to say obligatory goodbyes. She had acquired what she wanted. I never figured out what that was.

A BAND OF WILD MONKEYS

1982

I LURCHED BETWEEN SELF-DISCOVERY and self-destruction that first year in Japan. Sometimes, I had blurry, indistinct images of what I might become, and at other times, self-sabotage, and bewilderment. It was as if I had come to Japan at the bottom of a deep cistern. Sometimes I was able to scramble part way up, only to slip back down.

Toward the end of my stay in Osaka, I headed by boat to remote Cape Toi, a raised peninsula that jutted into the Pacific Ocean from the rural Miyazaki Prefecture's southeastern tip. At one point, it had attracted weddings, but the site had fallen on hard times of late. Why would anybody want to have a wedding in rural Japan when you could fly your friends and family to Hawaii? Some tourists still came, though, because caramel-brown wild ponies roamed the pampas grass that grew lushly on the sloped hillsides.

I had made no hotel arrangements in a country where nobody really wings it. After getting off the train from Miyazaka City, I switched to a bus to Ichinami Beach. I haggled with a boat owner to take me to Kojima Island to see the red-faced monkeys who were the only inhabitants of the island.

After pulling sweet potatoes out of the ground, they'd scurry over to the ocean and thrust the spuds up and down to wash the dirt off. I waited for the boat I had hired to return but it never came. Clouds rolled in from the sea and it suddenly started pouring, sending me sprinting off the beach into the deep forest, where there was at least some protection.

My highest priority was protecting my Sony Walkman, which had been playing Cat Stevens' greatest hits throughout my journey. "Wild World" certainly resonated with me on this trip. Realizing I had not eaten in hours, I pulled out *senbei*, salty crackers covered in seaweed.

Perhaps it was the smell of food, but I saw a set of eyes gleaming close by, then two more, and two more. Standing up, I broke into a run and in one motion was 20 feet up a Japanese cedar tree before I stopped to think. The monkeys had given chase and, of course, could have climbed the tree, but they turned away, bored.

That's where I spent the night, awake, and soaked. Some friendly tourists took me back to the mainland the next day and I resumed my journey south to Cape Toi. No more island side trips, I vowed.

I stopped in small villages for rice, miso soup and beer, and then resumed walking until I made it to the very tip of the peninsula and looked down at the sandy coastline circling the deep green hills, which were in turn framed by the cobalt sea and cerulean sky.

This one view was worth the monkey chase.

Atop one hill, I spied a black and white crescent on a

beach in one of the coves not so far away. Having nothing better to do, I found a path down the hill and went to investigate. Muscular vines tried to hold me back, but I pushed through. When I had made it down the hill and looked closer, I realized it was a whale carcass, once the size of a pickup truck. Its flesh had been picked by scavengers and what remained, desiccated by the sun.

After inspecting the whale, I lost interest and turned to head back up the trail, but there was now a young girl in my path. She was about my age, with swept back hair in a bun topped with a fuchsia hibiscus flower. She wore no makeup over her naturally glowing cheeks. On her young, taut body hung a blue *yukata* adorned with a white flower pattern.

"What are you doing here?" she asked in Japanese, slightly tinged with a southern Kyushu accent. She only then seemed to realize that, as a foreigner, I might not understand what she was saying.

We both looked up. In the distance, trampled earth reverberated as a group of five or six horses raced down a nearby hill for no apparent reason.

Her simplicity was elegant, and I was speechless for a moment. There was something more happening here, though. I said, "I came down to see the whale."

"It's not a whale anymore—without its spirit." She looked back up to where the horses were, but they were gone.

"What's that you're picking?" I asked pointing toward her basket half full of what looked like giant, vivid-yellow lemons. "*Hyuganatsu*. It's a native citrus fruit, kind of like grapefruit—only sweeter. They are a special Miyazaki fruit." On cue, she pulled one particularly plump piece of fruit off a low-slung tree.

Out of nowhere, a small paring knife appeared in her right hand, and she expertly cut the fruit into eights, and offered several to me. They were succulent, but tart, pulp spraying out of my mouth. Her motions were spare and efficient. Nothing was wasted.

"What's your name?"

"Kazumi. I live in the village by the ocean over that mountain. It's a bit far but the *hyuganatsu* grow big and sweet in this spot." A gust of wind blew off the ocean and a few strands of her hair came undone, dangling in her face. She put her basket down slowly and redid her hair, effortlessly twirling her hair tie around a neat bun and lastly making sure the hibiscus was properly situated.

Enthralled, I muttered, "I like your *hyuganatsu*."

"What's a foreigner doing on Cape Toi? We don't get many around here." Bending, she lifted her basket again.

"I, um, came to find myself," I stammered, immediately embarrassed by the idiocy (and truth) of my comment.

"So you've been lost," she said tauntingly and giggled as she swallowed another slice of the fruit. "Oh, well, it can't be helped," she said, resorting to the stock Japanese phrase of resignation.

We both were silent. Then she looked at the sun's height in the sky and announced, "I must go. Goodbye, foreigner."

She disappeared into the vines.

* * *

About a month before I left Japan to return to New England for my senior year of college, Atchan became my girlfriend. I told myself it happened by accident but if I was honest, I had been maneuvering toward this outcome from the moment I met her.

Throughout the first semester, we continued to meet in the central courtyard of Kansai Gaidai on the same bench where we had our initial conversation—even when the weather became cold and inclement at year-end. It didn't snow much but we often had to don heavy coats, woolen hats and gloves or mittens.

Ostensibly, the conversation continued around me answering her questions about Rhode Island and Providence College. The militaristic karate guys continued to run by in their bare feet no matter how cold. They never returned my gaze when I tried to make eye contact, but I didn't take it personally.

By the time early spring began to push away the winter, and the plum blossoms flashed their glory—a slightly redder shade than their more famous cherry blossom cousins—I detected a subtle opening, or at least I thought I did. I'd still never had a girlfriend before.

We went to Atchan's family apartment, which was a short bus ride from the school. The apartment, on a low floor in a big building, was warm and bookish. Her mother taught English for a living out of her house and sat on a *tatami* floor hunched over a lacquered table with a young boy facing her.

"I will go to America someday," the boy pronounced with a great degree of difficulty.

They looked up as Atchan and I entered the room. The mother's eyes narrowed, obviously sizing me up. "Okaasan, this is the Michael who I told you about," she announced.

Her mother's face went blank and then Atchan added in Japanese, "We'll both be in Providence College next year."

"Hello, Michael-san, welcome," she said in slightly formal Japanese, surprising me that we were not conversing in English.

Atchan served me some barley tea and cut up a Japanese pear. We ate and drank quietly while standing in the kitchen so as not to disturb the studies. After I finished, I laid my dish and glass in the sink, and was just about to squeeze some dishwashing soap on them when Atchan suddenly grabbed my hand. "We never use soap on dishes—it leaves a residue you just can't get rid of."

Now in fear of breaking other household rules, I suggested we go out and grab some snacks. I put on my blue blazer with the school karate club badge. After watching the club members dart past me on their masochistic bare-footed runs during the winter, I couldn't resist joining.

We walked around and gobbled up some street snacks. Atchan opted for *takoyaki*, balls of batter with bits of octopus; while I scarfed down *okonomiyaki*, cabbage pancakes smothered in mayonnaise and a sweet and sour brown sauce, which covered my whole face by the time I was done. After we finished, we said our goodbyes. I decided to walk home instead of taking the bus.

The next week, I invited her to join me for a visit to Iwafune Shrine, which was up a mountain from the town, Katano City, where I had lived with my homestay family. This small metropolis abutted the highlands, which I explored on long, punishing uphill runs. I popped Kenny Loggins or John Lennon cassettes into my Walkman to accompany me as I made my way up the meandering roads. Once I arrived at the shrine, I liked to stop, sit on moss-covered stones, and absorb the Shinto spirits, which I began to believe occupied everything around me.

There was no running with Atchan; we took a bus from Katano. Soaking in the lush countryside, our excitement soared the more we distanced ourselves from the hustle and bustle of metropolitan Osaka. The Amano River, becoming more and more pristine as we climbed the mountain, was a welcome and attractive companion as we neared the summit.

After the silence of the bus ride up, I was disturbed when Atchan immediately turned chatty as her feet hit the ground. We were so used to sitting on benches at Kansai Gaidai, it suddenly struck me we had never really frequented many other places. I hadn't seen her in different settings and therefore did not know the many dimensions of her personality.

Neither did she know mine and, at least around her, the

reserved, murkier side of me remained shrouded by the graciousness she was drawing out from me. I feared if she came to know the real me as I perceived myself, there would be no possibility of a relationship.

She had done more research on Rhode Island and her questions spilled out like the fast-flowing Amano.

"I'd like Newport, right? It's near the ocean, I think," she fired off the questions as she bounced and quickly stripped off her striped sweater, tying it around her waist.

"It's gorgeous; you should see the mansions," I responded, bragging, as if I had anything to do with building the mansions there. "Rich people built them. They're so opulent," I said, but then caught myself. Though Atchan's English was spectacular, she didn't like it when I used big words.

We entered the grounds of the shrine through a stone *torii* gateway. A golden rope dangled from the front. Other shorter stone posts with lush moss coats poked out of the ground, the ancient Japanese carved *kanji*, which marked them barely visible. We'd come on a weekday, so the number of pilgrims was far fewer than on the weekends.

"I'm going to be in Doer," she blurted out, bringing her hand to her mouth. I worried she was going to spit her tooth out again.

"The dormitory? PC has parietals, you know," I said. I could use this line of conversation to guide the chat to a desirable place.

"Pa—rye—eh—tal—z. I don't know that word," she said with the innocent, questioning look she always had when she didn't understand something in English. She was never afraid to ask.

"You can't be in dorm of the opposite sex past a certain hour. It's a Catholic school, remember?" A young family with small children eating ice cream out of plastic cups passed us.

We could now hear the crotal bell bellow out from the

shrine and spread over the grounds. I imagined it was beckoning me to make a move. Trepidation arose at the thought of being the aggressor. That was not a role I was comfortable playing in any human interaction.

Atchan was wearing very tight green jeans with a sheer white blouse covered in dripping black dots. She wore little jewelry and makeup, and her natural look was just perfect for her.

I playfully bumped her hip with mine as we talked about parietals. I reddened both at the touch of our hips and the thought of being in her dormitory room alone with her.

"Well, I don't think my boyfriend will be coming to visit me," she said, suppressing a pseudo laugh.

The shrine loomed in front of us—a dozen steps over crushed gray gravel.

"Why don't we pray? We've come all this way," I whispered, observing all the cartilage twists and turns in her ear before I put my mouth close to her.

We approached the small entranceway to the shrine, poured water over our hands using a wooden ladle and threw some coins in the box in front of us. This shrine's uniqueness stemmed from the fact that it was grafted onto a giant stone that was said to once have been a ship ridden by a god from heaven.

Interrupting the solemnity, I said in a low voice, "Maybe he won't be your boyfriend anymore once we get there."

I smiled. She paused and looked at me trying to figure out what I meant.

We stood shoulder to shoulder, bowed, clapped, and pulled the rope to ring the bell. As she did, a wind sprinted through the open sides of the shrine, sweeping back her hair and revealing the full, flawless symmetry of her face. Without hesitating, I kissed her. It was quick but wet, her heat lingering on my lips as I stepped back and opened my eyes. Momentarily unsteady, I floated back to the surface of my own life after being sunk in her.

She looked genuinely confused yet she had not resisted at all.

We went back to praying and then turned slowly like we were awakening after being someplace else and retraced our steps to the bus. We stopped at the entrance of the shrine to have some green tea and traditional *mochi*.

The kiss had added a sudden weight between us, and it was unclear whether it would meld us together or cleave us apart. As we got close to where we would part in Hirakata, she suddenly blurted out, "This is all so sudden. I gotta think about it."

I wondered if I had ruined what was becoming a great friendship. On cue, darker clouds gathered overhead. The clear day that began with possibilities yielded to uncertainty.

NO CHEERLEADERS IN CHINATOWN

2019

PERHAPS BECAUSE MY EARLY SHOPPING forays as Maeve were going relatively smoothly, I assumed I would slip seamlessly into Maeve in other areas of my life. I was sadly mistaken.

The disintegration of my marriage in 2017, which triggered my move back to New York City, was messy on many levels. I had not only split up from my wife Jackie, but I had been separated from my two boys. Then there was the loss of my town, Pound Ridge, a ritzy suburb 50 miles north of New York City.

Jackie is just over five feet with shiny brown hair. Often pensive and reserved, she never raised her voice when she was angry, but the edge in her tone could effortlessly carve up me or the boys when we crossed her.

In the twilight of 2018, nearly a year after I got sober, a degree of trust had crept back for Jackie—enough trust where she felt comfortable going to see her father in the U.K. and leaving me to watch Liam and Connor on my own.

I decided to take the three of us to visit my brothers in southeastern Massachusetts, near Providence. I packed a mixture of male and female clothing—nothing overly girly—including tight jeans, fitted sweaters, and heeled boots. And some makeup, which I, of course, wore lightly. I thought nothing of it. For three or four days, we had meals out and dinners at my brothers' while the boys lazed around by the big fires my pyromaniac brother liked to get roaring in his fireplace.

At a New England Patriots game we attended right before Christmas, everybody was festive, including the cheerleaders who danced and cavorted in red sequined skimpy outfits. It was frosty but not the bone-chilling frigidness we had experienced at Foxboro football outings in the past. I texted my new AA friend in New York, "I'm having a great time except I wish I could be down on the field as a Patriots cheerleader."

After I returned with the boys to Pound Ridge, I had to go back into the city for errands and decided since I was foregoing nail polish around my boys, I'd get my brows tinted and shaped. After spending another couple of days in Pound Ridge, I headed back to the city, just missing Jackie as she returned from the U.K.

As I stared out the window of the Metro North train bound for Grand Central Station, I let my body completely relax. Bonding with the boys had felt successful.

* * *

For New Year's Day, I had been invited to Chinatown for lunch with some friends. Part way through the meal, I got a text from Jackie.

"*We need to talk.*"

"I'm with some friends. I'll call later," I replied.

"*No. Now.*" That insistence was not typical of her.

I stepped out of the restaurant onto the crowded streets of Chinatown. Jackie was angry and for the life of me I could not figure out what I had done wrong. Immediately, fear spread from my stomach, engulfing my entire body. I was sober; this wasn't supposed to happen.

"I don't know what's going on with you, but I can't believe you subjected our children to it," she said, fury rising with every word.

"I'm sorry but I don't know what you're talking about," I stammered, feeling the old fear welling up from when Jackie used to confront me about my drinking. I looked up. The streets were filled with Asians enjoying an unseasonably warm New Year's Day.

"So, you didn't wear girls' clothes and makeup and do whatever you did to your eyes?" she retorted, daring me to deny a clear truth.

My heart sunk not just out of embarrassment but more because this was not how I wanted my children to learn about my wonderful new self. In my professional capacity, I would say I had lost control of the narrative.

"Do you want to tell me what's going on?" she demanded.

A German shepherd on a leash suddenly lunged at me and started barking loudly. Her owner, barely apologizing, pulled the beast away and I turned my attention back to the call. "Jackie—," I began clearing my throat, but nothing came out. Collecting myself, I tried again. "A couple of months ago, I realized I'm transgender."

I rushed my words because I didn't want to be cut off. "I was waiting to tell you guys, but I thought it'd be okay to wear some things that weren't too obvious."

Her reply was clipped and her anger undiminished. "Good for you, whatever. Well, they were obvious." This is not what I had been hoping for. I gazed down the road at the throngs.

I wouldn't have minded if that German shepherd came back and interrupted this conversation.

"Did you know the boys called me while you were in Rehoboth? They were very upset. Connor was crying," she exclaimed, jamming a figurative blade into me.

I was shocked. I knew my drinking had harmed my relationship with my sons, but I always felt we were close. "Why didn't they just ask me what was going on?"

"They felt trapped, and didn't want to offend you," Jackie answered, her voice softening for the first time. But she wasn't quite ready to rest her case against me.

"And what was that you did with your eyes?" she inquired, not able to resist the probing given the upper hand she had in this conversation.

I unconsciously ran a finger over one of my eyebrows. "I had my brows shaped and dyed."

Just when I thought we were getting to a more comfortable place, she dropped another unexpected explosive. "Liam said you were texting one of your friends about being a Patriots' cheerleader."

My stomach turned some more. I hadn't thought about him reading texts over my shoulder. It was a joke anyway—kind of. "I'm sorry, this is all new to me," I hurriedly responded.

This was met with silence.

"I'm doing my best to understand this whole thing myself. Can I talk to them?" A boisterous, obviously drunk group walked by, chatting loudly in their native tongue. I couldn't hear that well. I just wanted the conversation to be over anyway.

Jackie sighed. "They don't really want to talk to you." There was a pause and then she added, "I don't think you should come up for a while. They need to process this, maybe discuss it with their therapist. We'll talk again."

I headed back into the restaurant. The food was cold and so were my companions, annoyed that I had been out so long in the middle of what was supposed to be a festive meal. I didn't care. I was too overcome by what Jackie had just said on the phone.

* * *

Six weeks later, I was back in Pound Ridge, which in some ways, I still considered home. That day, I was dressed as a man. Skinny, neither fashionable nor unfashionable, receding hairline and a perpetual scowl that was my natural visage. The boys were downstairs, and I quietly walked up the steps, followed by the loyal black Labrador who used to be my best friend, to the bedroom I had shared with Jackie for fifteen years.

Jackie was ready to talk about Maeve. I was excited and petrified at the same time. She sat up on the far side of the bed, while I sat on the smallest piece of the bed I could manage.

We'd purchased the place cheaply, mainly because it was a hideous A-frame. But, as Goldman Sachs paid me more money, we fixed it up into a comely two-story home that fit in well with its natural surroundings. The original brown and orange wood siding had been paneled over in a sedate green. There had also been a garage built into a ledge that hemmed in part of the property. It wasn't palatial by any means but a comfortable enough place for the four of us, the dog and two guinea pigs.

After ten or eleven hours in the office, and two-hour commutes each way, I'd get home at 8:30 p.m. so drunk it was impossible to be a partner or father, though I didn't admit that at the time. Then I'd drink even more in secret after everybody scurried off to their bedrooms for the night. Lying in bed and gazing at the sharp cut of the ceiling dormers, I mused to myself, "I love this bedroom and if I keep drinking every day, I am going to lose it all."

I was right.

A victim of my alcoholism, our relationship had lacked intimacy for a very long time. But here I was, 18 months out of the house, prepared to tell the person I had loved longer and more deeply than anybody in my life that I had likely harbored something so secret during our marriage that it eluded my consciousness for more than 50 years.

"So?" she started in her crazy mixed British-America accent, looking at me to get the story going.

"This realization just happened in October."

The dog had jumped on the bed and pushed himself into me like he used to when I shared the bed with him and my wife.

"It just keeps growing. It's not gonna go away. It's here to stay."

"What about work?" she asked. She was back to being kind, gentle Jackie, which was her usual steady state. Behind her through the sliding glass doors to a small porch, the invasive bamboo I had planted over three seasons now stretched four stories high and swayed happily in the breeze.

"I'm not ready for that yet but I change clothes on my way out to go to AA meetings," I said, smiling a little for the first time.

"So, they all know? This must have been a shock to you. It certainly was to me," she said in her understated British way.

"I'm seeing a gender therapist," I explained, "or at least that's what I call her. She specializes in trans and has other trans patients like me who came out late in life. I like her."

The conversation was not uncomfortable, but it wasn't smooth either. I looked around the sparsely furnished room. There was one little dresser and two-night tables on either side of the bed, one of which used to be mine.

"Are you doing anything else?" I knew what she meant.

Hormones or surgery—the questions every cisgender person likes to ask.

"I'm doing hormone therapy."

She gasped. "Really?"

"I'm getting little boobies," I smiled and squeezed my breasts. "Do you want me to talk about my growing breasts?" I joked. I used this one all the time because it legitimately was one of my cherished topics.

"So," she continued. This was one of her favorite words to pause on. "This is serious?"

"Oh, yes," I declared. "The other stuff like operations—that's way down the line. It's not something I need to even think about now. I imagine it's something I'd probably want to do."

The dog rolled over and showed me his furry white belly and I reached down and scratched hard.

Genuinely interested and on a roll, Jackie followed up, "Do you have a name?"

I broke into a huge grin. "Maeve."

She smiled back. In a strange coincidence, Jackie's grandmother, whom she had loved, came to England from Cork, the same city where I was born.

Jackie's tone shifted back to serious again. "You've done a lot of damage to the boys," she said, not meeting my eyes. "Just when they were moving on from all those years you were a drunk, you spring this on them. It's a lot and it will take time."

The dog snorted twice, as he usually did after lying upside down for too long in the hope of an extended scratch.

I did understand. The boys had grown up with an alcoholic father in a home now divided by divorce. They were both teenagers and here I was tossing my new transness into their lives. Though the world was changing, and my children were liberal in their thinking, a trans parent coming out late in life is complicated.

"I know. We'll take it slowly."

Reflecting with some shame as I rode Metro North again, I thought about taking it slow. I had meant it when I said it to Jackie. But another thought chased it away.

She is unstoppable, and Maeve wants to move fast.

THE NOT-SO-GREAT GATSBY

1982

BY THE TIME I GOT BACK to Providence College for my senior year, Atchan and I were a full-fledged couple.

On weekends, we drove again and again to Newport on day trips. She couldn't get enough of it. A peninsula near the mouth of Narragansett Bay, Newport is surrounded by so much water that there is virtually nowhere you cannot see any. This place, which became very special to us, must have seemed very open to her after urban Japan.

One Sunday, we stopped at a store in the center of town and bought the kind of clothing Duran Duran might wear— tight pants with bulging pockets down the legs and sheer striped shirts. We also purchased used black boots at a nearby Army surplus store.

After parking, we strolled along the cliff walk, the opulent Breakers mansion to our right and surf smashing on the rocks thirty feet below.

"Why did you kiss me that first time?" she asked simply as we held hands and strolled, stopping frequently to look at the ocean or the mansions.

From where we stood, the sun was a couple of feet away from touching the horizon. It had an unimpeded path to disappearance through the clear sky. The sunset would be clean and fiery.

"Why do you think? I liked you," I said through a wide grin. I just couldn't stop myself from smiling.

"It wasn't really fair to my boyfriend," she answered, but it was clear she was teasing. We still never used his name.

We leaned over the railing separating us from a steep plunge into the sea. The surf was rough, and some spray leapt up and popped on our faces.

The vastness of it all struck me in that moment. I wasn't alone anymore, and the self-recriminations, though not gone, had become much fainter. I couldn't say I had begun to like myself, but hating myself less was a big improvement and good enough for now.

What if I were Atchan?

That couldn't be, I pushed back. I could really appreciate her though. That night, back in her dorm room, I gawked in fascination at her naked body. This was the first time I had done so from a purely aesthetic perspective. The lack of a penis, the bulging hips, the soft hanging breasts. They were exquisite. I didn't really feel my body when I was having sex.

Sure, I needed it to have sex, but I deeply wished to shed it like a snakeskin. Being genderless would do nicely.

Atchan brought out certain surprising traits in me. I found that I could be kind and generous, qualities I didn't think I had. For the first time in my life, I could be thoroughly relaxed around another person who wasn't one of my siblings. Before Atchan, the uglier parts of my personality had always been dominant.

My life had been cloaked in darkness, but now I was in an early morning haze. It certainly wasn't clear, but the sun was out there somewhere beyond the low-lying clouds. I reached for a shifting, amorphous fragment of myself but it joined the mist and was gone.

And then, in what seemed like an instant, all the progress I had made figuring out who I was oozed out of me, leaving me withered and bewildered. The war-torn part of myself was always there, intent on sabotaging any growth that flared from time to time. Its weapon of choice was always alcohol or drugs.

My drug use escalated for the first time in my life. I'd always preferred booze but I was also an addict who'd try anything if it were offered to me. I was only saved from becoming a heroin junkie because I was terrified of being arrested and locked up for life. A friend agreed to be an intermediary between myself and a dealer, arranging safe transactions involving speed, coke, mushrooms, and mescaline—anything that picked me up.

I even used drugs on the job. My uncle ran a security guard service and he had managed to get me a night or two a week on the shift that nobody ever wanted—the Saturday overnight. I worked at Rhode Island Hospital, the giant care facility in Providence where any Rhode Islander with anything seriously wrong with them ended up.

I went to work on Saturday night drunk and used speed or mescaline to keep me awake. Of course, once my shift finished, I'd have to drink to get to sleep. Luckily, there was a bar near campus that opened at seven a.m.

Out with friends on a weeknight, I ended up at a house and for perhaps the first time ever in my life, the pretty girl in the room was interested in me, at least she was that night. We kissed and fondled each other for a bit in the corner of somebody's apartment and promised to do it again.

My roommates were having coffee in the kitchen when I arrived home and paused to hear me discuss my evening.

Atchan, concerned about my wellbeing, had stayed over and, in the middle of my boasting about the night before, she walked into the kitchen. The twisted expression of shock, sadness and disgust distorted her face into something unrecognizable.

A month later, she befriended a member of the school track team. But I was so persistent in trying to win her back that she relented and kept me in her life.

Once I was in her dormitory room when the front security desk told her a guest was coming up, the track guy. She looked at me unblinkingly.

"You'll have to leave. I'm sorry."

She started rushing around the small room, picking up scattered clothes and handing me any of my belongings. She was frantic to prepare the room for the guy and that enraged me, obliterating all the shame I had just felt for so severely damaging the relationship.

But I stayed hangdog, which was the better recipe for getting sympathy and perhaps making the other side feel guilty.

"Okay," I said, monotonically. Head sagging, I raised myself from her bed where I had lain clothed.

"I'm sorry, but it has to be this way," she answered back authoritatively, opening the door, and beckoning me to quickly leave.

She didn't seem very sorry. I slunk out through a back staircase. The relationship was spinning down and getting closer to the bottom of the drain. I was shattered.

Fortunately, that year I had Deirdre, the sister whose bed I crawled into when I was young and couldn't sleep, close by. She had transferred to Providence College from Salve Regina in Newport. We rekindled our sibling friendship over dinners of pasta and grilled cheese at her apartment.

Deirdre was average size and pretty, with blue eyes and dirty blonde hair like mine. When I started feminizing myself decades later, I swore that I sometimes saw myself as her spitting image.

After listening to Van Morrison on the jukebox and drinking pitchers of cheap beer at the local college dive bar, Louie's, we picked up egg sandwiches from a silver truck on campus and headed down Smith Street to my apartment.

Once in my apartment, I led her through the living room and then a bedroom and finally through a window out onto the rooftop. The building I lived in was a three-story apartment, but it had once been a beautiful single-family house with an octagonal turret sticking up from the second floor. We sat next to the turret on the roof, which had a manageable slope, eating our sandwiches stuffed with egg, cheese, lettuce, tomato and mayonnaise. It was messy but provided a perfect coating for the stomach after the beers.

"Can I tell you something that's been eating me alive?" Peeling the aluminum foil from a sandwich, I opened my mouth to take a bite, but clamped it shut. This conversation was upsetting on many levels.

"You're going to anyway. Go ahead," my sister joked, but she was right.

"I've destroyed everything with Atchan." I could hear the whininess in my voice and though it was unattractive, there was nothing I could do about it. A group of drunk PC students looked up at us, branded us losers and gave us the finger.

"Why don't you just break it off?" Deirdre asked. She was always more rational and even keeled. She nibbled on her sandwich like the rabbits that had been her pets.

"I just can't."

"That seems like more a problem with you than her," she answered, hurling the large truth back at me. I wasn't ready to hear it or do anything about that.

I nodded but I had said my piece about Atchan. It was

time to move on to the real reason I had lured her onto my roof with an egg sandwich.

"Now that you mention it, I have something a little embarrassing to ask you," I whispered, pausing. I rewrapped the egg sandwich, having lost my appetite completely.

She looked at me, silently urging me to speak. Finally, she said, "Go ahead."

"Well, I think Atchan is going to go to the senior prom with someone else," I said staring at the ground below the roof. "I don't have anybody to go with."

"You must be able to find *somebody* else," she said, drawing out the embarrassment of this awkward moment.

"I wish I did. Would you be my date?" I asked my voice trailing off in humiliation at the end of the question. It was out, and now I just had to wait for her answer.

"Sure, I'd be happy to." The drama was over, and I breathed a sigh of relief.

I do not even remember what Newport mansion hosted the prom. I must have gotten really drunk that night because that's what I always did. Deirdre did yeoman's work attending the prom with her own brother.

After college, Deirdre moved to Florida. I went down for her wedding and to visit occasionally. Of course, I saw her at family reunions in Massachusetts but over time, the closeness that we had growing up and all the way through college diminished.

The Newport experience was moot anyway. By then I knew I was going back to Japan, which seemed to hold the key for me. I had found a trailhead, which had led to Atchan and I was determined to find the precipice of self-discovery. Would I jump or turn back?

ALL MY TROUBLES SEEMED SO FAR AWAY

1984

MY TICKET BACK TO JAPAN after I graduated from college was underwritten by the Japanese government. Chosen for a program which placed Americans and British people into rural Japan, I was expected to make guest appearances at middle and high schools in the hope of igniting interest in English.

Coincidentally, I was going back to a neighboring prefecture to Cape Toi, the place where I was chased by monkeys and encountered the unusual fruit picker. In Kumamoto, once again, I stayed with a homestay family, but fortunately the mother behaved herself, and so did I for most of that year.

On the way from the airport to the home where I was staying, I pronounced in lilting Japanese, "This is really countryside," which elicited laughs from the homestay parents, Hiroshi and Noriko. A third person, a dour school administrator whom I always addressed as Soga-san, was also in the car.

Riding clunky buses that hissed dark, noxious fumes, I crisscrossed the prefecture to all kinds of schools and regions from Amakusa, the fishing peninsula with aquamarine seas in the southwest, to the fierce volcanic region around Mount Aso to the east.

There were touching moments that made me want to celebrate. Many of the students were meeting a foreigner for the first time and it was an overwhelming experience for some. One student made me a stuffed doll version of me dressed as Santa Claus, with blonde hair, blue eyes, and a gold spot on one of my ears for the earring I wore.

These school visits took my drinking into the stratosphere. Japan represented the peak of my social drinking, with the following decades a steady slide toward drinking alone out of bottles filled with the cheapest vodka available. After I got sober, I told myself that these were my fun years of drinking, and they were to a degree. But I was already waking up after an abbreviated sleep, disoriented, with a crusty mouth, fantasizing about the most effective forms of suicide.

The first night of my stay in any school district, I was taken out for *sashimi*, grilled fish and rice balls. My night out in Yatsushiro, a town south of Kumamoto City along the coast, could have been anywhere in the prefecture. The wood-paneled drinking spot was warmed by happy human bodies suffused with beer, *sake* or that local brew I drank in Cape Toi, *shochu*.

"We Japanese are a shy people," announced a teacher I silently dubbed Red Face, whose whole body had turned crimson after his first glass of beer. I did not know the hierarchy, but he seemed to be relatively exalted in the pecking order.

I nodded. This was meant to be an education, not a conversation, I quickly concluded. There were four male teachers and one woman. She sat off quietly and slowly nursed one glass of beer the whole night.

Red Face-san slapped me on the back and filled my beer glass up again. I reciprocated by wordlessly gesturing toward him to down the rest of his beer so I could refill his glass. More and more men piled in, and the temperature climbed inside the restaurant, the only respite coming when newcomers lingered as they entered, letting in a quick blast of cooling air.

"You're a good foreigner," he said, lighting a cigarette. Everybody was smoking except for me and the poor woman teacher. I felt cheerful and friendly, as if I belonged. After we had feasted, it was time to go singing and we headed to a bar down the street. I entered a cave, with glinting half-empty whiskey bottles catching the dim light as we walked by, illuminating our way like votive candles on a church wall.

A more mature woman, who probably would have shown facial wrinkles in the daylight but appeared youthful and spry in the evening, came back with an almost full bottle that she said belonged to Red Face.

"Michael is our guest. Pour him some whiskey, Sachiko-san," Red Face barked at the woman. He was swaying and slurring a bit, but he clearly had no intention of stopping.

"Do you like Johnnie Walker?" Sachiko asked me kindly.

"Anything is fine with me," I replied, eliciting laughs from the other teachers who interpreted my comment as a willingness to drink anything for as long as the evening kept going.

Sachiko came by me to pour my whiskey. "On the rocks?"

I nodded as I drank in her perfume and gazed at her neck, which was white and long. If she noticed, she didn't show it. She was used to being leered at by drunken men.

She slowly and alluringly picked up single ice cubes with tongs and gingerly placed them in the glass and then gently filled it halfway with the amber liquid.

It was time for karaoke, which I was always reluctant to do because I had been told I couldn't sing my entire life.

Revved up by religious songs, I joined the church choir as a youth, but I was so tone deaf one of the nuns impolitely suggested I find some other way to serve God.

Red Face and his pals belted out traditional Japanese songs called *enka*, heavy on the theme of unrequited love. They also channeled their energy into flirting with the young ladies who fetched the half-filled whiskey bottles the men had previously purchased.

There were always a few English songs available and no matter how remote the village, I could always count on "Yesterday" by the Beatles. By the end of the year in Kumamoto, I detested that song.

That night, I slowly rose from my seat, feeling lightheaded from the *shochu* and whiskey as I headed toward the mic. Behind me was a small screen where the words of the song floated by, always at the appropriate speed. I had done this dozens of times already, but I was stricken with the feeling of isolation. *What am I doing alone in this remote place?*
Why am I up here, allowing myself to be subjected to insult?
This is all a recipe for more, not less, terror in my life.
The song began and the English words streamed. Two lines behind already, I quickly caught up. While singing, I reflected on the lyrics. *Yes, my troubles are here to stay.*

These outings grew to be so cookie-cutter that I became more adept at being a guest as the year wore on. Knowing what to say and do helped relax my hosts and made for more comfortable evenings. It was stressful and tiring, whether I drank or not. My reward at the end of the night at whatever inn I was staying at, was a sumptuous *futon*, laid out on the floor with soft white sheets, a light blanket and a thick covering. When done right, there is nothing that beckons and suggests a deep refreshing sleep more than this bedding.

The year in Kumamoto was one of equilibrium for me. I

didn't slide any further down the sinkhole I was fashioning for myself or get any closer to understanding who I was. In a way, it was a year of hibernation.

From the moment I arrived, Mount Aso pulled at me. I visited it again and again in my dreams. There was something yonic about volcanoes, the vaginal canals to the core of the earth spewing lava during orgasmic eruptions. During an earlier school visit to Aso High School, I had been driven up to the lip of the caldera, letting the sulphureous vapor bathe me in its stench and draw me to its source.

Inhaling deeply, I found myself inside the volcano looking over a molten lake. In the distance I saw a tiny speck on this igneous lake slowly moving toward me. The wait was interminable. As it moved nearer, I finally glimpsed a figure standing on a boat paddling. The boat had wooden ribs and a small mast with no sail. It could fit no more than one other person in addition to the rower.

As it neared, I could see that the rower was a woman with Japanese features, deep brown pools for eyes, high cheekbones, and white skin the color of pearls. She had the defined musculature of a man, but her facial features were soft and sad. Her hair was pinned back austerely with a lacquer hairpiece. She approached the shore and gestured for me to get into the boat.

"Don't set foot in the water," she warned ominously. "You'll boil alive." She dropped her oar and extended a cadaverous hand which chilled me upon touch despite the heat that was everywhere around me.

"I'm not going with you," I said, attempting to resist her insistence.

"Hurry up. We don't have much time." The urgency of her request compelled me to climb over the side and into the boat. I tripped but righted myself. She pushed the boat away from

the side of the fiery lagoon and set out for the other side, which seemed far away.

"Where are we going?" I stammered.

"To the other side." She was speaking Japanese with a Kyushu dialect.

"What's there?" I asked with trepidation, stammering through two words.

"You will know soon enough." She ignored me and steered the boat past whole rocks that had not yet been subsumed by the lava.

I asked meekly, "What did I do?"

She ignored me.

As we finally neared the other side of the lagoon, it seemed to be covered by a large orchard of cherry blossom trees, with delicate pink petals falling in a type of flowery shower. But no matter how many petals fell, the trees were not denuded— new petals grew immediately. As I got closer, I could see that the petals attached to the trees were engulfed in a pink blaze. And then I heard the groans.

Mesmerized, I asked, "What is this place?"

"Where do you think you are?" she answered back, unimpressed with the scene in front of us which she apparently had seen thousands of times.

"My name is Karon and my responsibility is to get people over here," she said, assuming formality. "Do not ask me what here is. I am just the rower."

I stared into her eyes, and they were suddenly dead, showing nothing. Now that she had stopped talking, I focused on the moans and whimpers.

I suddenly realized that there were only men here and was about to ask why.

Ash concealed the land nearby, choking off all vestiges of life. Near the crater, there was near silence except for an unnatural hissing. I turned away.

* * *

As my year in Kumamoto was coming to an end and I prepared to return to the U.S., I sat across from Atchan in an Osaka coffee shop. It was early June and the rainy season had just begun. The humidity was oppressive, the thick rain unending and the sun non-existent. Nobody felt particularly happy except the frogs that thrived in park ponds.

The coffee shop had turned its air conditioners full blast in an attempt to squeeze some of the humidity out of the air. The windows had fogged up, sparing us the scenes of people fighting the rain and wind, which pulverized their umbrellas.

"We have to talk," Atchan announced.

I had barely sat down and was not even comfortable yet. There were a lot of young couples smoking, drinking iced coffee, chatting excitedly. At least we'd have iced coffee in common. I slumped in my chair and felt my mouth begin to crease. Because she was my first girlfriend, I never had broken up with anybody. A young male waiter brought our iced coffees in copper mugs on a tray and placed them in front of us.

"Go ahead," I goaded her, hoping I could at least wring a little guilt from her. "Get it over with."

For somebody who had loved me, stayed with me during multiple international relocations and tolerated my derelictions, she was very businesslike, which I had never really seen before.

"I've met this musician," she declared and then went silent. "Change" by Tears for Fears was playing in the background.

Turning back to her, I tilted my head and ran my fingers through my perm. It was several weeks old, so the curls were not as tight as they were when they were fresh. Even though the air conditioning continued to blast, it was boiling so I removed my black leather jacket. Atchan seemed irritated by my fidgetiness. But I was about to get dumped and felt no obligation to help her feel comfortable doing it.

"And we've been talking about how white people have taken advantage of everybody—blacks, Asians," she continued.

The waiter came back to see if we wanted refills. I shot him a "leave us alone" glance and he slipped away. Smiling, I tried to make a joke and said, "I know I'm white, but I haven't ever done anything like that."

"Bob Marley hates white people, you know," she threw back at me.

This conversation was so insane, I quickly concluded I was helpless. She went on a little bit longer, but I was only half listening. I did hear the word breakup, though by that point in the conversation, I had already thrown in the towel without so much as a feeble protest. Rejection had always been my greatest fear and I went to great lengths to avoid being put into situations where being rebuffed was likely. This was the ultimate rejection and every one of my cells screamed *escape*.

I couldn't get out of Japan soon enough. I finished my teaching contract at the end of June 1984 and developed a plan to travel from Japan and meet my father and sister in Ireland. For a thousand bucks, I was going to make my way through Asia and Europe on Air India and eventually sync up with my family, where it all started, in Cork.

I went to Seoul first and ventured into the countryside, where English was little spoken, but the older Koreans dusted off the Japanese they had been forced to speak during the Japanese occupation and welcomed me. After an uneventful stay in Hong Kong, I was overwhelmed by the beauty of the palace in Bangkok but got robbed of all my belongings in Chiang Mai by a gang working in concert with a girl I was having sex with.

In India, the heat and crushing poverty of Delhi and Bombay led me to a travel office, which put me on a flight to Kashmir. I stayed on a houseboat, smoked a lot of hash and, when I got bored, hired a guide to take me around the Indian Himalayas for a week. I feasted on dal and naan and bathed in glacial runoff that stole my breath and threatened not to give it back.

Then it was off to Europe. While in Mikonos by way of Frankfurt and then Athens, I met an Italian girl and we traveled together for a while.

I gaped at the ruins of the Forum in Rome, meandered around museums in Paris, and strode into just about every pub I walked by in London.

I flew from London to Cork Airport, a small regional airport dwarfed by its international cousin, Shannon, in the middle of the country. When I went through customs, I had a beard for the first time in my life and wore a loose, traditional Indian outfit, which was purple, no less. I was filthy and emaciated from booze, hash, malnutrition, and constant diarrhea; and I probably stank. My appearance coupled with all the colorful Asian country stamps in my passport pre-ordained me to a full body pat down in Cork.

"You look disgraceful," my father said in disgust after I was released.

"I had to fit in with the locals," I shot back. At age twenty-four, I didn't have to listen to his shit anymore.

My sister laughed. "I'm not surprised to see you like this after some of the crazy letters you've been writing."

I had to share a bedroom with my father, which I did not enjoy. Once I got cleaned up, I realized he shunned bathing, and was the dirtier one.

Deirdre and I let him be the guide. We went up a hill to the Cork City Gaol, which had held political prisoners during the Irish War of Independence. Then we went to Cobh, a short distance away from Cork, where the *Titanic* made its last port of call. And of course, we visited Blarney Castle where I had to lie down to kiss the famous stone.

My father had not changed. He was taciturn and edgy in the morning but expansive into his second stout at Flannery's Pub, where I had used to sit on his lap as a child. It was a treat in a way because I got to witness him as close to being happy as I had ever seen him.

"See why I like it so much here," he said, showing his brown and crumbling teeth.

He put his arm around my shoulder. It was like a scarf of dead flesh, and I just wanted it off me.

MY NEW FAVORITE COLOR IS FUCHSIA

2019

THE GREAT WARDROBE CHANGE came about in the winter. For most of my career at Goldman Sachs, I commuted from Pound Ridge into the City, got off the train and jogged to work. My starting point station depended on how hung over I was.

I kept Hugo Boss suits in a closet at work, had them dry cleaned near the office, and changed back into comfortable sweat clothes for the commute home. The workout gear also served the purpose of soaking up the sweat that broke out when I started slugging vodka or flavored rum right after work.

But now, living in my own apartment on 84th and 2nd Avenue, I went to AA meetings almost every night on the Upper East Side. Because I didn't have time to go home between work and meetings, and I couldn't bear the thought of not dressing as a girl after having been in a straitjacket of a suit all day, there was only one answer.

I spent the day as Clark Kent and on the way out of Goldman Sachs I transformed into Wonder Woman.

One day in late November, I began to get squirrelly around 5 p.m. just like when I was drinking, but instead of vodka I needed lipstick. Before I left the privacy of my office, I applied eye shadow, mascara, and brow definer. Looking at myself in that small, pink hand mirror, I felt I had struck the right balance: I was already feeling better because I had begun to transform, but not enough for anybody to really notice.

One of the assistants tapped on the glass window of my office. I hurriedly pushed all my makeup into my top drawer, stood up and opened the door.

"Do you want to take a call from Bloomberg?"

"Of course," I answered, wondering if she had noticed. I could have sworn she looked at me funny, but I couldn't be sure. After the call, I went to the men's room, where I changed into pink corduroy pants, a bra, a pink sweater, and black high-heeled boots.

After going through my email one last time, I carefully packed my belongings, keeping accessible what I needed for the final touches to my appearance. Obviously, minimizing my time transforming in the men's rooms decreased the likelihood that somebody would walk in on me.

The office had cleared out early so I did something I didn't normally do on my floor: I put a light coating of deep red lipstick on and headed for the elevator. A slow-to-come elevator used to enrage me when I couldn't get out of the building fast enough to get some liquor in me. It was almost as bad today because I stood exposed in the hallway with lipstick on and no place to retreat.

The elevator came and I rushed in. Good, I said to myself, only one other person was present. Feeling relatively safe, I dutifully took out my iPhone because that's what people do on elevators. Peeking up at the other occupant, I realized he was a senior investment banker whom I had been friendly with. We often talked about career and family while going up to Bloomberg for TV hits. Since we both had experience living in Asia, we also swapped stories about our adventures there.

He wouldn't look at me and I did not know if that was because he was just busy answering emails or he thought I was some type of freak with makeup on.

What's he thinking? Why is he ignoring me?

Suddenly the grains on the tan ligneous walls of the elevator began twisting and the car started getting smaller and smaller. I really needed to get out immediately.

Once the door slid open, I sprinted out to the second elevator I had to take down to the first floor. This one was larger and always full, so it was easier to sink into the corner and be anonymous.

With thick wooden stalls and higher quality marble, the bathroom on the first floor of Goldman Sachs' headquarters was grander than others in the building because client events were often held on the first floor. This bathroom, the closest to the exits, was rarely occupied at six or seven, when I was leaving. I put on my wig, added to my makeup and donned a frilled yellow blouse.

Rushing toward the exit, I nearly bumped into a Goldman Sachs hospitality person who I didn't really recognize though I probably passed him several times a week. He did a double take when I went by; I hurried into a stall and loudly slid the lock.

I crept out of the auditorium and willed myself to the last obstacle, the turnstiles, after which I was free of Goldman Sachs and worry. The same two security guards stood at the card swipe station. Initially, when I began this complex dressing dance, I avoided looking at them and kept my head down, but they were always respectful. After a couple of weeks, I would catch their eye and nod.

Today, I looked them in the eye and said, "Goodbye, have a nice night."

The next complication was the subway. New York could feel like a small town at the most inopportune times.

On Wednesday mornings, I varied my routine, and this is what really set tongues wagging about me on my work floor. I had started going to a ritzy yoga studio on Madison Avenue on the Upper East not too far from my apartment. I became enamored with yoga's basic principles of being present and serving others, which meshed well with the teachings of AA. Having run for so many years, my hips were in constant pain and yoga also held the potential of prolonging my running career.

That is what got me in the door in early sobriety before I realized I was a woman, but once I came out socially, I couldn't stay away because the studio was full of girls being girls in colorful tight yoga clothes. Of course, I had been and continued to be sexually attracted to women, but I was also gynophilic, attracted to all that is feminine. This had been true my whole life, but I had never had the consciousness or vocabulary to describe it.

Now I wanted to be like them and be among them. Buying clothes didn't faze me anymore and I strode semi-confidently into an Athleta between my apartment and the studio to buy my first set of women's yoga clothes.

I could already feel the tight spandex cradling my body as I walked around the store. Ignoring anything subdued—black, blue or gray—I made a beeline for a section that had pinks, oranges and greens.

Figuring out sizes was still a problem. More assertive as well, I asked one of the women working in the store, "Am I a large or medium?"

"You're probably somewhere in between; why don't you try both?" she answered thoughtfully.

She hadn't flinched and I had her undivided attention. "Would you come back to the dressing room area and tell me which fits better?" I asked, a little imploringly.

"Of course." She looked around to make sure there weren't too many other customers and followed me to the back where there were a half dozen dressing rooms with piles of unwanted yoga clothes.

Still a little boyishly rough taking off and putting clothes on, I fixed my hair after each wardrobe change and opened the changing room door modestly. The temperature in the dressing room seemed to rise during my clothes odyssey, climbing to the point where zit-size beads of sweat broke out on my forehead.

"Medium definitely," she concluded with conviction after seeing me first in a large pair of pants.

I left with a matching fuchsia set of yoga pants, a top and a sports bra; a white pair of pants with a peach and gray dot pattern; and a baby-blue long-sleeved shirt.

I wore the fuchsia getup to a Sunday evening class the next day. Part of me wanted to go shirtless, with just a sports bra. Having been on estradiol, a form of estrogen, for a couple of months, I already had breast buds worthy of a teenage girl going through puberty. I was certainly bolder, but not daring enough yet to go shirtless.

For the Sunday class, I put my mat smack in the middle of the room amidst all the girls, breaking my pattern of practicing up front by the teacher. There were a couple of guys, but they were inconspicuous, hidden by a dozen girls, some in tight, sexy sports bras, others in more baggy clothing. As we went from warming up into more difficult side planks, crow position and head stands, I snatched glimpses of myself in the mirror. I was at one with the beautiful feminine throng.

Most of the classes I took were on weekends, but there was a Wednesday class starting at 6:45 a.m. with a teacher I really liked. Since I was so used to going to yoga dressed as a girl, I couldn't bring myself to dress any other way. My favorite outfit was the fuchsia top and pants, to which I'd add gray high-heeled boots and the fake white fur coat I had bought with my daughter.

One day after one particularly strenuous Wednesday yoga session, I was walking to work through the Oculus. A young black woman stopped in front of me and politely said, "Excuse me."

"Yes?" I looked her in the eye, which still took a lot of effort for me to do with strangers.

"I was just admiring the way you move through your space," she said. Then she turned and disappeared into the crowd.

I muttered a thank you. Nobody had ever said anything like this to me before and, in the moment, I was stumped by the meaning of her words. But as I started thinking about what she meant, I became convinced she was saying that I looked comfortable with who I am.

As the full import of her words took root inside me, I stopped and smiled. Catching my reflection in a shop window, there I was, moving through space.

* * *

People in Goldman Sachs' headquarters don't gawk. If you're appropriately dressed, they notice and ignore you. If something is off, they'll steal a glance and register distaste with a slight turn of the head or a puckering of the mouth.

Head held high, I entered the building, avoiding nobody's

gaze during the two elevator rides up. I felt invincible in my yoga gear, fur coat and heels—it was an armor I never had, protecting me from doubt and imagined critical looks. Then I reached my floor.

A senior woman in our marketing department, who I had a cool relationship with, eyed me up and down when I passed her in the hallway on my floor and then looked down to fish her ID out of her pocket. She didn't greet me.

I realized this getup was a bit too much for somebody who supposedly was still a male. I was starting not to care. For that matter, the clothes-changing routine, which I had found elating a couple of months earlier, was really starting to irritate me.

Why do I have to do this every day anyway?

ASLEEP AT THE WHEEL

1985

AFTER HAVING EXPERIENCED THE WORLD on my way back from my second stint in Japan, I was in Rehoboth again. Though it was 1985, it was as if Dorothy, her world now black and white, was returning from Oz. Diversity in my hometown consisted of being either Irish or Azores Portuguese. The few Jews, Protestants or blacks stood out like small islands amid the sea of Catholics.

My plan was to go to graduate school for Asian studies. A newly purchased, second-hand Ford Mustang took me to multiple jobs, including my first job as a freelance journalist. That is, until I fell asleep at the wheel in broad daylight. Sharply jerking the wheel when I woke up and realizing I was drifting off the road, I sent the car into a rollover. I slipped out of the ruined vehicle completely unscathed and waited for the police to arrive.

One of the neighbors sidled up to me and said quietly, "I do hope the driver is okay."

I nodded and moved away.

* * *

I was establishing a pattern: Whenever something didn't go quite right, I returned to Japan. This time, after the accident, I had been back in the U.S. for less than six months, as opposed to the year I spent between the first and second times there.

Once back in Tokyo, I settled in West Shinjuku, a rundown, working-class residential area that seemed a world away from the hustle and bustle of Shinjuku's more active entertainment areas.

Three of my good friends, who had been on the government teaching program, had also established themselves in that neighborhood: Timothy, a lanky Minnesotan with a taste for flamboyance; Jenny, a working-class Chicago girl who loved a good laugh; and Dennis, who was from Massachusetts and expressed himself awkwardly whenever he talked.

I started off working in Tokyo for ASA Asahi Sankyo, an English language factory, which gave hour-long lessons for mostly adults. Their main office was in Shinjuku, so I had just a 20-minute walk to get to work, which allowed me to avoid the professional shovers outside crammed subway cars. My friends Timothy, James, Tony, and Helen worked there, too. We'd get paid about 40 bucks an hour and worked five or six hours a day. That was certainly enough to get a reasonably priced apartment and go out to eat and drink every night. What else does an expat in his mid-20s need?

The place was run by a husband-and-wife team of snake-oil vendors—the husband was a greasy haired chain-smoker, but it was the wife who really managed the place. It was reputed that the school only existed to gamble upfront payments in real estate, which was in the midst of a speculative bubble.

To make their Ponzi scheme work, they had to keep people coming in the door. The school advertised extensively and when potential students came in for demos, the most attractive and silver-tongued teachers were put in front of them.

I had a pretty good conversion rate (just over 50 percent) of getting people to sign up, particularly young, single Japanese women who still lived with their parents and, for that reason, had a lot of disposable income. This was a most coveted group.

I never considered myself particularly good looking, but I certainly wasn't ugly. I had dirty blonde hair, blue eyes and, though of average height in the U.S., was tall by Japanese male standards. Though I drank copious amounts of beer at night and ate loads of fried foods, I ran regularly and was still young enough to keep the weight off.

It was common for the foreign teachers to flirt with the young women at the front desk, who had the distasteful title of front companions. These women were the first line of offense for ASA Asahi Sankyo. Dressed in blue or black dresses and white blouses, they blurted out the most formal Japanese whenever a new potential student walked off the elevator.

I caught one girl, short at just over five feet, eyeing me. Her hair was down to her jawline, cut perfectly; her cheekbones high and prominent; and her posture impeccable. My eyes grabbed her name from her nametag, Mikako, when she wasn't looking.

One day, I followed her out of work, pleading sick to avoid my last two classes. We strolled over to Shinjuku Chuo Park, the one near my house, and had a light, safe conversation. Soon we were dating, which meant she mostly came over to my apartment after work.

I knew she lived in a swanky neighborhood in Kichijoji but I was shocked when I walked up to the building at the address she had given me when she invited me over for the first time. It was a towering Shinto shrine with an enormous courtyard. Such emptiness was an extreme luxury in a place like Tokyo.

She apologized for not telling me sooner that her father was a Shinto priest, and his occupation allowed her family to live on these spacious shrine grounds.

She brought me into the living quarters to meet her mother, who was in the kitchen, putting the finishing touches on our lunch, which consisted of a pitcher of cold barley tea, *onigiri* rice balls with pickled plums and some seasoned slabs of *tofu*.

We took our meal out to a stone bench on the shrine grounds, and I gazed at the entrance to the shrine, which was framed by six wooden pillars and capped by a sloping green roof that I assumed was copper.

"What a gorgeous—," I started but paused because I saw something noisily pushing the bushes aside.

Mikako's eyes followed mine, but she apparently didn't see anything.

"Mikako, do you have dogs or cats around here?"

"We have cats to kill the mice but they're usually inside." Taking a bite of her rice ball, she exposed the purple plums on the inside. "They're probably *tanuki*."

Then out of the bushes I had been watching, two small mammals, their faces dirty from foraging, jumped and raced across the courtyard so fast my eyes couldn't keep up.

"What's a *tanuki*?" I asked.

"I think you call them raccoon dogs in English—they kind of look like raccoons but they're bigger," she said growing slightly more animated. The turn in the conversation had broken her nonchalance.

"They're cool."

"*Tanukis* are known for bringing prosperity," she said, assuming yet another personality—that of a bookish educator.

She paused again, looked to where the *tanuki* had run and when she didn't see anything, took another bite of her *onigiri*, dabbing her mouth daintily with a handkerchief.

"Speaking of prosperity, I am about to extend some to you," she said, trying to keep a straight face but unable to stifle a smile.

I put my lacquered lunchbox down and stared at her. She had me where she wanted, hanging on her every word.

"Do you want to be my date for National Coming of Age Day?" This was such an honor she just let her question dangle, already knowing how I would respond.

"Need you ask?" Coming of Age Day on the second Monday in January was only one of the most exciting nights in all of Tokyo, when girls who had just hit 20 or were about to hit 20 walked around Tokyo in stunning *kimonos*.

* * *

At her side that night in an Issey Miyake plum-colored suit, I stood for photos in the shrine courtyard and drank in her perfume as if it were coming from me.

After bowing before the shrine and expressing gratitude for our good fortune, we had a *sake* toast with her father and nibbled on dried squid.

An Italian dinner in Harajuku was followed by drinks at the Sky Bar in the New Otani, the most expensive hotel in Tokyo. I surprised her with a room there for the night.

If only I were wearing the kimono *with the taut* obi *constricting my breathing, the long garment limiting me to tiny steps at a time, and thick makeup whitening my face.*

For weeks after, I conjured up an image of myself going to Gion, the traditional section of Kyoto, which was still home to the remaining geisha. A professional aesthetician would put my hair up, smother my face in heavy makeup and methodically layer on me the individual pieces of silk fabric that comprise a *kimono*. My opulent silk outer garment was royal blue with the pinkest cherry blossoms; my obi was so gilded it looked like I was wrapped in gold filament. Finally, my hair was crowned by blush-colored flower adornments. Gazing at myself in the mirror before I left to wander Kyoto's many temples and shrines, I gasped.

Blinking at the mirror, I saw only a sad man looking back at me.

WELCOME TO THE PLEASUREDOME

1986

MIKAKO AND I DID NOT LAST MUCH LONGER, but I took the memories of that night and tucked them deep inside me for another day. In desperate need of companionship, I befriended a fellow Asahi Sankyo teacher, a tall, thoughtful, albeit morose, Brit named Tony. We met in an izakaya chain in Kabukicho called Kitanokazoku. I loved the grilled rice balls and fried *tofu* while everybody else seemed to opt for *yakitori*, the grilled chicken on a stick.

"Where were you before Tokyo?" I asked, more jocularly than usual. The two beers I had pounded had gone right to my head and warm friendliness circulated inside me. The place was loud and full of young Japanese on a budget.

"Kashi," he said inaudibly, or the word was muffled by the noise in the drinking spot and Tony's British accent, which was posh and subdued. We were sitting at a square bar, really a thick piece of wood heavily blemished by cigarette burns. Inside the square, the chefs grilled our food and poured us beer and *shochu*.

"Hoi," one belched in response to a customer shouting for an order of grilled octopus. The chef fished a small, whole octopus out of a plastic container and thrust it on the grill. It hissed as if still alive and voiced its extreme discomfort.

Picking up a grilled rice ball, I inspected it to see if the grains, saturated with soy sauce, had just the right amount of burn. Concluding that it did, I took a big bite. I was stalling for time as well, trying my best to figure out what exactly he had said. I made an educated guess he'd said, "Kashmir" and that gave me an opening.

"I was there last year and it sure is mountainous," I said, drawing out the "sure is" part.

Tony went along though his eyes narrowed, showing the slightest trace of puzzlement. His chicken skewers basted in a dripping sauce had just arrived and he gingerly raised one to his mouth, bending forward to avoid soiling his clothes with the greasy sauce.

"It's a little way from the coast but the fish is still really fresh,' he pointed out, looking toward the door as he was expecting Helen, another teacher at the school and his girl-friend, to pop through at any moment.

Now I was baffled; I hadn't seen any fish at all up in Kashmir. I resolved to take back control of the conversation and steered it back to the mountains. "I had a guide and hiked through the glaciers," I boasted. My fried *tofu* came, floating in a sauce with ginger and chopped scallions.

"I'm not sure we are talking about the same place," he said. "Why don't we resay the names?"

"Kashmir."

"Kashiwa," Tony clearly said. It's a city not too far from

Tokyo. We laughed and became friends thereafter.

Friendships between foreigners forged this way in Tokyo often became enduring. They had to because, no matter how long a foreigner lived in Japan or how well he or she spoke Japanese, they would never be considered a native.

Just as I was liked, for the most part, by Japanese people because I was a white Westerner, the fact was I would never be fully accepted. This was a great relief for me, though a constant source of anguish for other foreigners who were frantic to be considered a native. It meant I didn't even have to try.

At the ASA Asahi Sankyo Halloween party, Tony dressed as Dracula, Helen as a flower and I as a cheerleader, with huge fake breasts, a tight white sweater, and a short red skirt. The teachers all did themselves up and paraded through the neon glowing entertainment part of Shinjuku. The point was to also have the students put on costumes and frolic with the teachers to learn the nuances of adult Halloween but most of the teachers, including myself, didn't want to have anything to do with the students.

The freedom and anonymity Halloween afforded was totally liberating, just as it was all the other times I had previously dressed up as a girl for this holiday. On these occasions, it was as if I molted, and the Michael hide fell to the ground.

I had been a baby girl, a lascivious enchantress and, in an eerie foreshadowing, one year in Massachusetts, I dressed as a half-man and half-woman, which now in retrospect I wish I had taken a deeper look at. But by this point in my life, I accepted everything as it was and did not believe I had the power or ability to reorient myself toward a different path.

On the weekends, we went to discos, the gaudiest one in the 1980s being the Maharaja in Roppongi, the large entertainment district in Tokyo. This dancing palace arose just as Japan was flexing its economic power around the world.

Every market in Japan was only going one way, and everybody felt rich.

My look had evolved to androgyny. My hair was permed up top and chopped short in the back and sides. I added a second piercing ear on my left ear to complement the one my brother had given me during college, courtesy of a sharp, hot needle.

I wasn't sure if this guise was going to work for me. I just knew that every attempt up until now hadn't seemed right. It was as if I was searching for the right skin to cover my core, but I had to rip them off because they never were suitable.

My friend from Minnesota, Timothy, became my stylist, applying my blush, eye shadow and lipstick. When I was alone, I brought out the makeup case, put some on and lay on my futon naked, trying to erase from my mind who I was and create somebody new. The erasing was easy, but the inventing was near impossible.

I didn't dare tell anybody, which wasn't very hard. Secrets were familiar, intimate, and a huge part of my life, particularly the concealment of the true amount of alcohol I drank and the severity of the hangovers I had every morning.

Timothy, an aspiring fashion designer, and I prepped for a night at the Maharaja at his apartment, blasting Duran Duran and Scritti Politi. Standing in the middle of the *tatami* mat room, well-lit by a traditional Japanese *chochin*, or round paper lanterns, we chugged a Polish vodka called *Zubrowka* and dressed up while chattering away.

My choice for the evening was punky red tight jeans with straps, and a silk white and black striped shirt topped off by my black leather jacket. Though I had the impression others viewed me as stylish (for the first time in my life), that's not how I regarded myself.

Timothy came up with the idea of accessorizing the chest hair I hated—by this point, the list of detested features included my penis, receding hairline, all body hair, fat thighs, thick calves, and bulging shoulder bones—by shaving a lightning bolt into it. While I appreciated his handiwork, I'd never shaved there, and red welts immediately sprouted where there had been hair. The sweat that rained from me when I danced made my chest one massive itch.

"*Kimi*, how's it working out with you with that schoolteacher?" I asked as Timothy applied the bright red lipstick. I puckered my mouth, still not used to having a covering on my lips.

We sometimes used rude and inappropriate Japanese words for "you" as terms of affection when addressing each other.

"*Omae*, to tell you the truth, I've been going out with her for three months which is a long time for me," Timothy said, pronouncing some words a little bit flatly. He had successfully discarded most of the vestiges of his Midwestern roots, but the accent cropped up from time to time. We were good friends but not so close where we would divulge our true, deep feelings to each other. Conversations twisted into vast and varied terrains because once we started going too far down a path, one of us changed topics.

"You know, I'm going to get my fashion design business up and running," he announced suddenly. This had been an obsession of his, but now it seemed closer to reality.

"I'll be one of your first customers. I would be proud to be." I took a long sip of my vodka. Putting it back down, I stared at the lipstick's imprint on the glass.

Timothy grew animated as he typically did when talking about his fledgling business. "I have a tailor in Hong Kong all set to go. All I have to do is send the drawings and material specifications, and he will make them cheaply." He put some mousse in my hair to get the curls just right and I winced when he tried to pull through a kink.

"I have some designs here if you want to see." Then he

stopped fixing me up and pulled out a hard cover book with drawings of super thin people in idealized forms.

Wanting to support his new venture, I chose two extra-long, buttoned shirts, which were meant to flap outside the pants; a pair of extremely flared black pants that would have made David Byrne proud; and some colorful bright blue and orange pants with distorted triangle shapes that were loose fitting and seemed more like pajamas. I was always looking for something interesting to wear to the discos.

"I've been keeping a diary. One day I am going to make all of this into a book. I don't know if anybody will ever read it," I said bending the conversation in a different direction.

Part of me wanted to look at myself in the mirror but I knew anything I liked about my appearance would be overshadowed by what I didn't like.

"I will," Timothy chimed in.

I wanted to tell him how much I loved putting on make-up as he brushed on eye shadow and mascara. But instead, I blurted out, "I'm thinking of studying ventriloquism."

"That's not something I expected you to say."

To be honest, the idea had popped into my head only the day before. This was a time in my life when it was difficult to follow a straight path. Tangents veered me away from whatever I was focused on at the time.

Though I didn't admit it to myself, there was no way I would ever follow through on studying this craft. If I was honest, it was the disembodiment, temporarily transferring my personality to something else, that appealed to me.

"I think I'm done with the disco pickup scene," I continued, twisting the flow of the conversation yet again, after getting scant response to the ventriloquism comment. Timothy nodded but seemed unconvinced. We finished getting ready and hopped in a cab to Roppongi.

Maharaja's entrance was defended by concrete black panthers ready to pounce and corpulent fake pillars all designed to contribute to a sense of opulence.

The strobe lights immobilized us as we entered, and the bass beat attacked. Frankie Goes to Hollywood's "Relax" was blasting just as it was every night at discos around Japan in the mid-1980s. The throng of boyfriends smoking and drinking blocked our access to the bar, but we persevered. Their girlfriends were watching themselves dance in floor-to-ceiling mirrors that revealed their disinterested, emotionless expressions.

After a quick drink, Timothy and I just pushed onto the floor and started dancing, moving toward anybody who interested us. Frankie was telling me to "Relax" as I split off from Timothy and edged my way toward a Japanese girl my age; I began dancing with her. We snapped our heads back and forth, and every third snap or so, we looked at each other. Globules of sweat formed on my forehead like hot springs bubbling out of my skull. I wiped them off and smiled at the girl.

We were leaving the disco together 30 minutes later, after stopping at a table filled with her friends who obviously objected to her departing with the "bad" foreigner. Following a couple of hours in a nearby love hotel, an exchange of phone numbers and a hasty goodbye, we parted. But that night, I had the insatiable thirst of an alcoholic that would not be sated by one encounter. I was back at Maharaja without considering why I was there. A Singaporean girl with a taste for expensive martinis pulled me out of the disco to a posh bar and then a different love hotel.

The next night I found myself with a Russian woman I met on a train platform who planted a big smoky kiss on me for no reason. On Sunday, with Marvin Gaye providing background, I had sex with a fourth women that weekend, a spoiled American girl living in Roppongi with her rich parents.

That night I took the subway to Shinjuku and began the twenty-minute walk to my apartment. Sometimes when I drank too much on a weekend, I talked to myself, creating an alternative me in an alternative place. As I neared home and passed an urban concrete river, I imagined myself in the mountains of Nagano, stepping into a bracing mountain stream to cool off after a dip in the bath at a hot spring resort. The dream began:

I would have gone a little bit farther into the river than I had last time because I wanted to feel the current, but not so much that I would be carried away. I submerged in the bracing water and slipped a little on the slimy rocks.

I heard a grunt and looked up at an overhanging rock ledge where there was a small creature. At first it looked like a monkey, but it had no fur. With webbed feet and hands, she (and I somehow knew she was female) was either green or brown with greasy skin that glinted in the dark.

"I like going back and forth between the hot bath and cold stream," I said, for some reason not surprised by the sudden appearance of this creature or my desire to communicate with her. Looking down, I saw the shallow water carrying leaves eddying around my legs.

"So do I, but these onsen *people don't like me to get in the bath," she said. Looking closer, I now categorized her as a cross between a turtle and a monkey. On top of her head, there was a ridiculously large dish platter. Munching on one of the three cucumbers she held close to her breast, she looked down on me with some degree of interest.*

"What are you doing out here?" she said in a voice distorted by her lizard throat.

I decided to turn the tables and start asking the questions. "Who or what are you?"

"I'm a kappa and I live around these parts. I swim around

in streams, come out, and collect cucumbers," she said, look-ing at the remaining two vegetables and deciding whether she wanted to move them from her chest.

"That doesn't sound like much of a life mission," I said, mocking her.

"Sometimes I help the humans; sometimes I hurt the hu-mans. It depends how I feel." She looked like she was trying to shrug her shoulders even though she didn't have any.

I looked at her curiously.

"Don't worry. I already decided I am not going to harm you," she said, sensing my relief. But almost immediately, she shifted to a verbal volley of her own. "I could say you're already doing a fine job harming yourself."

She avoided my eyes and said nothing more. How she could know anything about me given she just hung out in mountain rivers?

We stared at each other for who knows how long. "I can only tell you something's wrong, but I can't tell you how to fix it."

I thought I might have seen a tear glinting in the moon-light, but it might just have been a drop off her head bowl. She threw the last bit of her remaining cucumber into her mouth and without looking back at me, dove into the stream.

I was not looking at a fresh mountain stream in Nagano, but an urban watercourse. If I continued these boozy one-night stands, I risked collapsing. But this was another play-book I was missing: How to stop.

* * *

At the same time, something novel was happening in my sex life. Up until this time, I hadn't had much exposure to the gay community. When I was young in Rehoboth, my parents would drive the family out to Provincetown, the gay mecca at the tip of Cape Cod. We'd get rock candy, saltwater taffy, and bags of shells. Of course, we also gawked at the gay men in leather holding hands.

Since many of my friends in Tokyo were gay, I spent a good deal of time in Shinjuku Ni-Chome, the gay quarter, or Second District, as we liked to call it. My gay friend James and I cut a deal. Sometimes he'd compromise and go dancing with me and other heteros, as he liked to call us, and other times I hung out with him in the district.

There were cramped watering holes and small dancing spaces sprinkled around the gay district, and some of the gems were deliberately difficult to locate. The place we always ended up, however, was the Kinsmen, a lovely name for a special place. It was on the second floor of an unremarkable building, right at the informal border of the district. A gay Japanese couple with impeccable taste decorated and ran the bar. Whenever I entered, I could not help but gape at a huge floral display in the middle of the place, which was surrounded by tables on three sides and a bar on the other. It was the kind of place you could take a straight girl on a quiet Sunday night because she would think it was cool.

This was a time of experimentation for me, not a lot, but certainly some firsts. I spent several pleasant nights cuddling with a Black airline steward whenever he had layovers in Tokyo. I also went home twice with a very intense Italian man, but he was too aggressive and spoiled any chance there was of me getting aroused. It was probably impossible anyway, given how I felt about my penis.

"I think it's great you're experimenting, Michael," James said, popping peanuts into his mouth at a cramped, dark Ni-Chome bar called Propeller Drive.

"I'm not sure it's going to work for me," I said, looking toward the other end of the bar. Two Japanese men in their early thirties kept snatching glances at James and me. It was unclear whether they were attracted to us or disdainful.

Hailing the bartender, a tall effeminate man who always had a smile on his face, I ordered a vodka martini and cradled my head, something I did when I couldn't figure things out.

"Just keep investigating, and you'll get to the right place," James said. He was always so kind and reassuring. When I didn't respond, he quickly pivoted. "Let me tell you about the cute boy I met the other night."

Totally unmoored, I latched onto whatever I bumped into. But there was intention in pointing the vessel toward Ni-Chome, though I still did not yet have the capacity to understand why.

THE MOMENT OF TRANS

2019

I stood outside of Goldman Sachs' headquarters at 200 West Street across the highway from the rebuilt World Trade Center on May 28. It was early morning though the night was still holding on for a bit longer. I had just had a tense, jittery ride on the subway and a ten-minute walk from the Chambers Street subway station.

Though I had worked for Goldman Sachs for 15 years, I was about to enter my workplace for the first time. This was my initial day at work as Maeve Chevonne DuVally, a nervous transgender woman who had thought herself a man for the first 56 years of her life.

The spark for coming out at work was a panel sponsored by Goldman's LGBTQ+ Affinity Network on how to make the workplace more comfortable for transgender people. The week before, an email announced the event to be held in the auditorium near where I changed clothes every day.

I felt compelled to go to the panel in broad daylight

dressed as Maeve, in the lime-green longish sweater I had bought at the Loft.

Listening to the three out trans people—one from Goldman Sachs and two from outside—talk confidently about how they dealt with discrimination and the work they did to help other trans people, my reluctance toward being out at Goldman Sachs evaporated like a puddle on a summer day.

An openly gay managing director I knew slightly had ridden down with me in the elevator and soon after, he spied me in the auditorium after I had changed into Maeve. He emailed me, "Congratulations." I stayed for the reception afterwards and met other gay men and lesbians.

"What did you think of the panel?" one masculine woman in a suit asked me.

"I want to be on one of those panels someday," I answered, surprising myself. "You never know who in the audience might be helped by what's said."

No one asked me anything about being transgender. They all talked to me as if I was one of them and they already knew me. I decided on the spot that now was the time to come out at work.

I called Lisa, the British person in Human Capital Management who was assigned to help me with my transness at work, the next day. I had put her on notice in January that I was transgender but added I wasn't yet ready to come out.

I got to the point right away. "I want to come out."

"Great. When?" Her "game on" attitude fortified me.

"How about after Memorial Day weekend? I like the idea of kicking off the summer in my right gender." That was just six weeks away but now that I'd decided to come out, I wanted to do it as soon as possible.

"Of course, first we'll need to tell your manager," she said unequivocally. I felt my breath intake. The idea of sitting with

Lisa, who was kind and clearly on my side, felt completely comfortable. But sitting in a room with Jake Siewert, my boss who I wasn't personally close to, or other senior people at Goldman Sachs, was intimidating.

"Should we do it together?" she asked, reading my mind. I wanted to wrap my arms around her.

"I'd like that." After 15 years, I knew my way around Goldman, but this was my life, not some company reputational issue, I was dealing with. The stakes were even higher.

"We have to start thinking about who else we need to tell ahead of time," she said, turning businesslike. "We have enough time, but six weeks is just going to fly by. Are you excited?" she asked, smiling through the phone, I could tell.

"Nuts," I nearly yelled.

We divided up the internal people between us; the reporters, the main external constituency I dealt with, were left to me. There was always the possibility that some reporter we told ahead of time might decide to do a story.

In addition to the posting lists, we identified all the technical issues, like name changes in email that we had to figure out. There were bound to be some unexpected glitches, but we agreed to sort them out as they arose.

One did. Right before Memorial Day weekend, I suddenly realized I had to deal with the Goldman gym in the building where I worked out every morning. Remembering the bathroom wars raging in some states, I was sickened by the thought of Goldman Sachs' women feeling uncomfortable because I was in the women's locker room.

Lisa and I came up with the idea of a dry run on the weekend when very few people were working out. I went dressed as Maeve early Saturday morning when the gym had just opened, and nobody was likely to be there. I worked out quickly and rehearsed how I would cover the not so feminine parts of myself and how I could shave my face at home, not in the locker room. I could make this work.

Whenever I needed fortifying, Lisa was my one big ally. On the Friday when we were trying to figure out the locker room, I confessed my misgivings. Lisa responded in a rougher British accent than usual. "If anybody gives you trouble, send them to me. I'll take care of them."

Two weeks before my coming out day, the *New York Times* said they wanted to profile the experience.

* * *

"Good morning, Emily," I greeted the *New York Times* reporter who would shadow me for my first day in the office as Maeve and for a couple of subsequent days.

"How are you feeling?" She sounded sympathetic.

"Out of my mind."

"I'm sorry I'm intruding." Emily said. Tall with short, cropped hair, she had an apologetic way about her along with a touch of social awkwardness that I sometimes saw in myself. I was drawn to her and pleased she would be writing my Goldman Sachs coming-out story.

I had intentionally arrived at work at 7 a.m. because I wanted to meet Emily outside the building and to be in my office before everybody else appeared. We entered; I checked in my guest, and we went through the same turnstiles I had crossed hundreds of times as my male alter ego and as somewhere in between for the last seven months.

I had put my Maeve DuVally nametag on my office door on Friday when I left for the day, and it was still there greeting me as I walked into my office. My Michael DuVally nametag had been tossed into the trash where it belonged. I went to login. My login "mduvally" was fortunately the same, but when I got into the system and looked at my emails, they were to "Maeve DuVally." I felt a smile come to my face.

The Department of Corporate Communications at Goldman Sachs was located on the southwest side of the building on the 29th floor, so we had a panoramic view of the lower Hudson River, New York Harbor and the Statue of Liberty. At this time of day, the sun was rising on the other side of the building and its exquisite rays were bouncing off the glass towers in Jersey City just across the river. The effect could be blinding even in the weak morning sun.

The *New York Times*' photographer started snapping photos of me positioned against some indoor glass with blurred images of the Jersey City skyline projected onto it. She smiled ever so slightly when she reviewed them, and I suspected there might be some special shots in there.

I was wearing a black pantsuit with a striped tight-knit top, which shamelessly flaunted the small boobs, which had sprouted courtesy of my hormone therapy. Those were good choices, but my judgment failed me there. I had opted for the seemingly ever-safe black pumps though I had never worn them outside my apartment or for more than five minutes at a time, never mind a whole day.

To prepare for the day, I had spent a good part of Saturday at a high-end nail salon on the Upper East Side of New York, getting a gel manicure and pedicure in my new favorite color, fuchsia. Lash extensions completed my salon preparation.

The next day, I met my friend Deborah at the flagship Bloomingdale's shop on 59th Street where she worked. We'd talked a little bit beforehand, and she was prepared with a wheeled rack bursting with dresses, pantsuits, and blouses in every color imaginable.

I had suggested the clothing brand Theory and Deborah didn't disappoint, spending hours advising and dressing me. I'd never spent more than a half hour in a clothing store, and I was both grateful for her help and overwhelmed at the thought of trying everything on. This was the first time I bought professional women's clothing. I also did not know my sizes and I had no choice but to buy something I could wear for my first day at work.

"I thought the changing rooms over here would be better. Nobody ever uses these ones," Deborah said in her usual soft voice.

The first floor of Bloomingdale's, swathed with jewelry, makeup and perfume stands is a beehive of activity, but I looked around here and we had the place almost to ourselves.

"They're perfect," I said, smiling and realizing for the first time that shopping could be an enjoyable experience.

I peppered Deborah with questions.

"How does this look?" I tried on my first blouse.

"Is this supposed to be so tight?"

I put on a blush-colored Theory dress and matching jacket and pirouetted in front of the mirror smiling uncontrollably. There were matching pants as well.

"That looks so good, Maeve." Deborah might as well have been applauding from the grandstand.

"I'm not going to wear this on the first day, but this just might be a dress I can get comfortable with," I said, surprising myself. When I entered the store, I was dead set against buying any dresses because they seemed a higher risk than pants for making me look weird.

"It's about a thousand for the three together; that's a lot," Deborah said neutrally.

"I'm getting them."

Deborah's views on what fit me and what my style might be heavily influenced what I selected.

I was determined to buy enough work clothes to wear something different every day of my first week. The four-hour saga ended in success, though failure dogged me at every step of the way. I fretted I would tear something expensive; become entrapped in tight blouses and have to be cut out; and get entangled in dress linings like a flapping cod in a net. Finally, I had had enough and pulled the plug on the operation.

In addition to the blush-colored ensemble, I purchased a black pantsuit with a skirt, a blue pantsuit, a couple of blouses and an ochre-colored dress. In the end, I didn't care how much it cost; I just wanted to get out of the building and out onto the street into the fresh air.

Reveling in my success, I was also taxed emotionally. I had been sober at this point for 16 months and known I was transgender for seven months. I had been unable to look at myself in a mirror for 56 years; I couldn't suddenly get completely comfortable trying on clothes in front of full-length dressing room mirrors and another person for four hours.

My hair was another matter altogether.

I had two wigs and I opted for the longer blonde one on my first day of work, and though it had been washed and styled when I took it home for the first time, I had no idea how to make it look comely on the first day. I was condensing the decades that most women had taken to learn how to groom themselves into days or sometimes just hours.

The wig hair was thick and hot on this end-of-May Day and the hair kept falling in front of my eyes, blocking my side vision. I couldn't think of any way to fix that. Between the wig, shoes and care I took not to rip my new, expensive clothes, the sheer number of things that could go wrong with my appearance seemed endless and terrifying.

And I was already confused.

Did I want people to fuss over me and compliment me or just leave me alone and treat me like nothing had changed since Friday, even though everything had?

My colleagues began to trickle in and congratulate me. On my appearance, women mostly told me I looked nice, which I liked. I went back to my office, a non-descript box with a blonde desktop and cabinet where the workstation rested. But Emily's fly-on-the-wall journalism made this a day without refuge.

She was giving me space, but I was in sensory overload already.

An assistant I knew from the executive floor who had seen me walking to my office sent me an email saying I looked *amazing*.

A friend who had watched me struggle all those years with my drinking and sense of self-worth, popped her head into my office. She was the first person at Goldman I had confided in very early on.

"Of course, you look good," she said, whispering to me. "But what I noticed is your smile," she said, adding, "I've never seen you smile like that."

That just made me smile more. I was already adapting to the new reality. Each time I tried something for the first time, there was distress, but once I had a successful first experience, I was fine from then on.

"As long as people don't treat me like an oddity," I said, catching my reflection in my office's glass wall and fancying what I saw.

"Sometimes, I wasn't sure you were going to make it," she said.

"Well, I really *made* it, didn't I?" I thanked her for everything.

Mid-morning, I received a gorgeous bouquet from "my friends in commodities." This was the desk that trades oil, gold and other commodities and was considered royalty because most of Goldman's senior leaders at the time came from that area. I knew that though the card implied multiple senders, it was one person, Ed Emerson, the rumpled British head of the desk, whose direct manner and blunt exchanges belied a big heart.

The gifts continued to roll in. It seemed as if everybody wanted to let me know I was accepted—something that itself was hard for me to accept.

Katie, another out trans femme at Goldman Sachs in New York, wished me well and said I was top of mind: "I feel extremely proud to know you! Congratulations for transitioning!"

My appearance that day was the product of a natural evolution as I watched, learned, and experimented over the previous seven months. Separate from my exterior, I knew enough by now to recognize it was the seemingly minor internal realizations that were really the key to the whole experience. When I responded to the congratulatory messages, I did not just say, "Thank you," but added that the support of the sender was very meaningful to me.

And I meant it. I had never in my life expressed myself in such an effusive way. It just seemed right. That day, there was no blowback—only love and acceptance.

Surely, it couldn't last forever. Or could it?

PART TWO

STRENGTH

"Good and evil both increase at compound interest. That is why the little decisions you and I make every day are of such infinite importance."

— C.S Lewis, *Mere Christianity*

GIZA, NOT GINZA, IN TOKYO

1985

WHEN I MOVED TO TOKYO for my third stint in Japan in early 1985, Jenny, the Chicagoan, and I had the good fortune of living next to each other in a concrete and metal heap called the Kobayashi Mansion, which was anything but. The owner, Mr. Kobayashi, had a circular protruding gut, two discolored front teeth and a perpetual smile on his face. Sometimes his shirts, which he wore tight, would slide up and expose his stomach. He seemed to spend most of his days striding aimlessly around the neighborhood, gut thrust forward, with his hands behind his back.

His mansion was four stories high, with the first floor occupied by a dark drinking establishment called a *snakku*, that we assumed his wife ran, though I don't think I ever met her. I give him credit—he was open-minded. Not every Japanese landlord wanted the trouble and misunderstandings that sometimes came from renting to non-Japanese.

The neighborhood where I lived in Nishi Shinjuku was severed by a tributary of the Kanda River, which was concrete-lined and coated by whatever liquid flowed through it. The stench from the river battled daily with that from a nearby *gyoza* factory, which perfumed the neighborhood with garlic and pork 24 hours a day.

While I was still looking for apartments, Kobayashi brought me up to see a unit on the third floor, which was a typical size—that is a six-*tatami* bedroom and living room, a kitchen and dining room, with a wooden floor and of course, a bathroom with a colossal tub.

"Notice the *tatami* mat is new," he crowed, but I already knew that from the smell, which is a similar scent to hay, only muskier.

"And we get a lot of sunlight through these back windows because the house next door is small," he said as he pulled a toothpick out of his pocket and began scraping off the seaweed that speckled his teeth.

A porch was accessible through sliding glass doors, but it was not the type of place to loll in the sun. Once I moved in, I hung my clothes out there but it just faced another ugly, low-slung beige residential mansion. And, when I was sometimes not of sound mind, I leapt over the barrier to Jenny's porch naked and let myself in to have a beer and a chat.

"You're not going to get a better deal this close to Shinjuku," he said nonchalantly, now using the same toothpick to dig out the dirt from under his nails. Sixty thousand yen a month wasn't bad. I earned that in three or four nights at the English language school.

I took the apartment and three months later, I had a mini rat infestation. Kobayashi came up and helped me lay traps for the rats that had taken up residence in my apartment. I never saw them, but their feces pellets announced their constant presence.

This was the first apartment I stayed in for any length of time and I can't say I had a good sense of how to decorate. Quite randomly, the décor of my room was determined by a decorative blind I bought on a whim adorned with a sun descending on an Egyptian pyramid, which was encased in a halo of purple and pink.

"Wow, look at those pyramids, just like Egypt," he exclaimed, as he turned and placed a trap by my refrigerator.

I decided to run with the Egyptian theme, so I bought a luxurious and expensive sand-colored wool carpet to cover my *tatami* mat floor.

"What happened to the rug?" he asked, gesturing toward a red splotch about the size of a flattened possum.

That addition to the motif came unintentionally and somewhat painfully. On New Year's Eve when Timothy, Jenny and I went to a club with unlimited champagne, I came home more inebriated than usual and knocked over and broke a delicate vase. I then proceeded to step on it, gashing the bottom of my foot. Too drunk to care, I waited until the next day to get stitches, but in the meantime, blood pooled on my new carpet.

"Wine. You just can't get it out," I said, dribbling the words out because this lie was blatant and hard for me. There was little risk though because there was no way he was going to challenge me. He probably already thought of me as certifiably insane.

His eyes narrowed further when he surveyed the five palm trees arrayed in no particular pattern around my apartment. They were between six and eight feet high and the plastic containers that held them were obviously old.

"Where did you get those?" he pried. I must have blushed. Before my time in Tokyo, I had never really stolen anything in my life but for some reason, my moral compass had stopped working. I picked them up from in front of coffee shops and lugged them home sometimes when I was drunk.

Because they were outdoor plants, I awoke to grubs, centipedes and ants crawling around my *futon* the next day. I lied again, saying, "One of my friends just left Tokyo and had me take them."

"Is that so?" he said, using that phrase which fully cloaks the intent of the questioner.

"What's that?" he inquired pointing toward a mannequin, which I wrapped in toilet paper to create the impression I had a mummy in the room. I didn't bother answering because I didn't have a good explanation.

At night, drunk and spinning in bed, I listened to Mike Oldfield instrumentals over and over and imagined myself buried alive in an Egyptian tomb. I was falling again down a waterfall of vodka and self-hatred, and I didn't know how to make it stop.

I was a dedicated letter-writer to my family members, particularly my sister Deirdre. Words gushed out of me like the blood from my slashed foot. In one, I described wrapping a belt around my neck, cinching it and feeling the blood drain from my head until I was on the point of passing out—and then doing it again and again. I also wrote that I laughed uproariously at this game.

Then I really crashed and burned for the first time in my life. The drinking, the confusing self-discovery, and the meanness of the one-night stands caught up with me. I felt my nerves coiling around my torso and the more my anxiety climbed, the more constricted they became. Malignant concerns visited me from the moment I woke in the morning and bade me good night if I was fortunate enough to get a fitful night's sleep. I honestly didn't know that alcohol only made my condition worse, so I drank around the clock on weekends, hoping to pass out and get momentary relief. I lost my sex drive entirely.

It was a Saturday during the rainy season and the world above continued to urinate on the world below. I opened another large bottle of Kirin and poured it into one of my black glasses. The foam spilled over the edge, but I didn't care.

I just lay on my bed naked, not troubled by my neighbor whose window was about six feet away from my sliding glass doors. The only exception I made to my nudeness was to lay a dirty washcloth over my penis. In my state at the time, seeing it might have tipped the scales to stark-raving lunacy.

I hadn't eaten until I forced a couple of pickled plum rice balls down. Fearing that any food I ate would make it harder to get drunk and find oblivion, I had been avoiding meals.

Making matters more ruinous, the local shrine in Shinjuku Central Park was holding its annual festival. There was joy in the air outside as middle-aged men in *happi* coats bounced the *mikoshi*, or portable shrine, up and down as they parted oceans of people hoping to get a glimpse. Octopus balls, cabbage pancakes, beer and *sake* were everywhere.

I seethed at the rejoicing around me. How dare they when I was so miserable? Just because I seemed to be having fun at night, my underlying self-disgust was always nearby, reminding me of its presence. It was unremitting during the day, and I looked forward to the evenings and weekends when I could douse it with alcohol and make it just a little bit fainter.

Increasingly, there were times when heavy drinking no longer worked for me—to still the negative voices, to feel like I belonged, to sleep, to escape utter befuddlement. But on this day, it wasn't the inability of alcohol to soothe me that was pushing me closer to insanity. It was a high-pitched flute recording playing from speakers attached to cement telephone poles, as if boring into my head, telling me I was worthless and needed to die.

I gave up and let despair spread through my entire being.

THE UNFATHOMABLE

1988

LIFE BECAME SLIGHTLY MORE BEARABLE after several months, probably because I mostly stopped going out and cut down on my drinking. I tried to throw my energy into running and writing. Reading Henry Miller at the time, I set out to do in Tokyo what he did in Paris.

One cold December night, Timothy managed to drag me out to The Kinsmen bar. Wind pushed us up the staircase until Timothy opened the door to warmth and we entered with a whoosh. After we sat down, I had my eye on a young woman sitting with a group of friends on the other side of the room. She was wearing designer black, and despite being heavily made up, I could tell she had a natural attractiveness.

Timothy noticed and asked, "Do you like her?" Judy Garland was belting out a song in the background.

"I guess so. She's kind of pretty," I said with a faint enthusiasm. Nobody, including Timothy, knew what was going on inside me.

"Why don't I get her over here?" He had no doubt he wouldn't be successful. His lanky frame bent over the table talking to the woman as her friends leaned in to listen. They looked over at me and started giggling, which didn't mean terribly much.

Timothy returned with a broad smile. "She'll be over soon."

The three friends feverishly discussed this development but there was no sign of the girl coming over. Finally, she stood, broke free from her friends, and came over to sit next to me in a chair we had pulled over.

"Hi, I'm Michael."

"I'm Michi."

Shortly thereafter, I got my first real job in Tokyo, as a translator for a Japanese securities company, Meiko Shoken. Medium-sized Meiko couldn't compete with the "Big Four" Japanese securities companies, but it didn't need to. Since every stock in Japan was going up in the mid to late 1980s, all it had to do was piggyback on the recommendations of the larger brokerages.

I was the only foreigner with the company in Tokyo and a contract employee to boot. Lacking a sense of belonging, I asked to be converted to lifetime employment and my request was accepted. I was transferred from the international division to research where I translated reports into English and wrote some original reports in Japanese. One of my proudest moments was passing the broker license test in Japanese.

My monthly pay was cut to a level commensurate with other full-time employees, with some (but not all) of the cut made up by the annual bonus I would receive. Now, on the short end of cash, I made the critical mistake of moving into the company dormitory in the Tokyo suburb of Nishi Funabashi, a drab barracks-style edifice where I slept and ate dinner prepared for us—and "us" was all men—by some older women.

The atmosphere inside the company for its one foreign employee was stifling and the living arrangements felt like a regression to childhood. I needed to get out.

I found my exit in the form of Kyodo News, Japan's equivalent of the Associated Press, though judging by the ruin of the headquarters building in the shadow of the U.S. Embassy, it had seen better days. I then jumped at the chance to work for a new financial wire service, which had a decent-sized and growing office in Tokyo, Knight-Ridder Financial News. This also allowed me to move back to Tokyo, which I never should have left in the first place.

Michi began staying over at the apartment I rented in Hiroo, a ritzy section of Tokyo. The building was modern concrete and the back porch hung over a lush bamboo grove, which tossed out *thunks* that sounded like cracking ice whenever the wind blew through. The rent was a little too high for a journalist's salary, but I felt I deserved it after escaping from the dormitory prison.

Michi introduced me to her father, who lived in a one-room apartment, and we bonded over *shochu*, which he used to buy in the same kind of giant brown bottle that *sake* comes in.

"The father likes you," he said, referring to himself.

"I like you," I replied, choosing the only possible response.

The window was never open, and the small room was enveloped in a cumulous cloud of cigarette smoke but so was every place back then, so we just accepted it.

Michi rarely spoke up during our early courtship unless I did something that offended her. I didn't know what she thought of the relationship, nor did I know what I thought about the association, for that matter. All that became moot or very important because within a half year of our initial meeting she became pregnant. After some heated conversations, we decided to keep the baby and get married.

Despite my disdain for the Catholic church and the damage it had done to me while a child, I never considered having my wedding ceremony anywhere else. Christianity is not widespread in Japan, and we quickly realized our best option was to get married in a church affiliated with Sophia University, a private, international college founded by a Roman Catholic religious order in the early 1900s.

Michi was five months pregnant on our wedding day, which we tried not to let cast a pall over the occasion. I had to smile when we were taking our pre-nuptial Catholic education classes and were instructed on the benefits of the rhythm method of contraception. I looked at Michi's bulging stomach, and thought, *That ship sailed long ago.*

The pregnancy did not deter us from having a memorable ceremony at Sophia's chapel, requisite photos in the gardens of the New Otani, followed by a reception in a bar in Roppongi, which we rented out for the night. It was dinosaur-themed, on my wishes. We gave all the guests small pewter dinosaurs as party favors, but the best part was Timothy and I had spent hours making a giant papier mâché triceratops piñata that contained all kinds of gifts and treats for the guests.

I remember Michi's relatives opening the envelopes full of money received as wedding gifts and cursing my friends who hadn't given as much as they thought they should have.

After the wedding, I took my parents and little brother (born when I was 16), who had come over for the ceremony, to Kyoto for sightseeing. Between making sure we were never far from McDonalds for Ryan and a bar for my father, I was run ragged. I still don't know why they came and a part of me believed it was for some other reason than to share a special moment with me.

Our daughter, Myla, a mewling bundle topped by thick black hair, was born in a hospital with a cool Roppongi address. In 1991, I hit the age of 30 and decided that if I did not leave Japan, I would be in danger of becoming the dreaded lifer—a foreigner who had lost the ability to socially integrate back into the society from whence they came. Knight-Ridder had an opening in Washington D.C., and I jumped at the opportunity to see if I could make it as a successful journalist in my home country.

Japan was over for me despite my new Japanese family. I didn't know when I would get back to the one place where I felt I fit in by not fitting in. With this move, whatever chance I had to find out who I really was evaporated. I was going to have to try to be normal.

CORK PROUD

2019

AFTER MY FIRST OUT DAY AT WORK in May 2019, I trained my attention on the *New York Times* article. News features have a life of their own, which ebbs and flows depending on the prevailing priorities of the newspaper. Given I was the main subject of the story and cooperating, the *Times'* reporter Emily kept me informed about where it was in the writing and editing process but sometimes, I didn't hear from her for days, which would make me anxious.

As mid-June arrived, the story was getting close to the finish line—I thought it could have come out any day—when Emily called saying they had hit a snag. Some editors who had worked on the story felt that there was a disconnect between how I described my self-loathing and transgender realization.

"You talk about how you never liked yourself and then suddenly one day you realize you are transgender," Emily explained in her kind way. She added, "There is just something missing here that we have to do a better job of explaining."

"Okay, let's just you and I talk and figure this out," I replied. I certainly knew how to set ground rules. This was going to be an intensely personal call, but I'd already given her so much intimate material.

"We've already talked about how I used alcohol to try and offset the fact I hated myself, right?" I said, recapping. I nervously twisted the long cord of my office phone. My confession was over, I had thought, but here I was having to lay even more of myself bare.

"Without recovery, I never would have come out," I said definitively, hitting my stride a bit. Looking out of my office window, I glanced at the clouds lazily floating over New Jersey and became momentarily lost in their slow movement across the skyscrapers in Jersey City.

"That helps," Emily said, beckoning me through the phone to continue.

"We can't print all that though," I cautioned.

So, we began a process of negotiation, because this was *The New York Times* and once a story in this paper is out, whatever is printed becomes fact for its subject. After discussing with people in my recovery network, I told Emily she could mention in the story that I drank excessively for much of my life. That seemed to solve the problem. Now I was on tenterhooks for the story to publish.

On Thursday afternoon, June 20, I got a call from Emily telling me the story was a go online for morning the next day.

My colleague Taylor sent the story at 5:42 a.m. Friday morning to our global media relations team. The outpouring of support and encouragement I received in the wake of that article's publishing was a potent antidote to the isolation and dejection I had felt from the earliest time of cognition.

* * *

The story literally altered the course of my life.

In the months afterward, I received a bevy of invitations to speak publicly, the likes of which I had never experienced. It was unbelievable that people actually wanted to hear about my coming out experience. More importantly, the story helped put me in touch with other transgender people in corporate America who were in various stages of coming out.

Of the 300 or so emails I received that day, at least 200 were congratulatory messages. I answered each one individually and personally in direct proportion to the thoughtfulness put into each message.

I was cheered that all our senior executives and traders in the securities division whom I had worked with for many years had taken the time to reach out to me. Somewhat curious to me, however, was the immense silence on the subject from people I knew in investment banking. But I let that thought go. Too much good was happening that day.

One message that especially warmed my heart was from a former journalist colleague who was also from Cork (Ireland). He said I had made Cork proud.

By the end of the day, I was caught up on my responses and I went to bed exhausted, but with unbound enthusiasm for the next day. Saturday morning brought another 20 messages, but they started to peter out by the end of the day. I completely forgot the story was coming out in print because real-time online news was all that seemed to matter to people in markets these days.

But the *Times* had one last surprise for me. Mine was the lead story in the Sunday Business section, with the main photo of my face taking up nearly half a page. The reporter who covers Goldman for Bloomberg texted me early Sunday, expecting that I had already seen the print version. Lazing around, I had to put on clothes and trudge out to the local newsstand. When I saw the story layout and how big the pho-to of my face was, I bought ten copies for myself. The print story triggered another 50 or so messages that Sunday.

People reacted to me and treated me differently after that article. I have never been so convinced of the power of jour-nalism and storytelling. Of course, I was immensely grateful, touched and emotional. For most of my time at Goldman Sachs, I tried to do my job, but I had been in serious pain and had the anchor of alcoholism strapped around my waist.

When I came out, the universe shifted for me, and I was filled with hope and courage that I could be a person with a purpose.

WHITE NOISE

2019

SEVERAL MONTHS AFTER I HAD MY TRANS EPIPHANY in 2018 but well before I came out at work, a nurse who worked for Goldman Sachs came back with a recommendation for a therapist. Michele specialized in transgender patients and had ample experience with trans like me who had come out later in life.

"Michele comes highly recommended, but we know nothing about her firsthand, so please let us know if you like her," the nurse politely requested.

Through the years, I had had several therapists and I had wasted their time and my money because I had refused to tell them I was drinking. Why should I have? They would have just told me to stop.

It was strange making a pilgrimage to her office on the Upper West Side of New York, a place had I lived from the time of my journalism fellowship starting in 1993, through the courtship and marriage to Jackie, to the purchase of our first apartment and birth of our oldest son, until our decision to leave the city shortly after 9/11. This had generally been a time of happiness and possibility for our young family, only to turn sour as I marched toward destruction once we moved to Westchester.

I came in makeup and women's clothing the first time I met Michele, and for this time only, without a wig. From that moment forward, I was a runaway freight train, constantly seeking to up my game in terms of my outward appearance. Some of my women friends gave me constructive advice such as recommending I eat more slowly and how to apply blush and eye shadow less heavily while others were incredulous that I was not using facial serums and exfoliating daily. I could only assimilate so much at a time.

Michele's office was on a quiet side street in the West 80s close to Central Park. It was in the basement of a brownstone, with a warren of offices for other therapists, complete with what seemed like several dozen white noise machines littering the corridor like rat traps.

By session three, we began getting into the good stuff.

"I kind of feel like I don't have trans street cred because there's no long history of girl thoughts," I said, starting the session. I was on a large stuffed couch and Michele faced me, legs crossed, on a chair across the room. The lighting was subtle, from lamps arrayed around the room.

"The trans community isn't one size fits all," she said with compassion (but not too much compassion, which would have been off-putting to me). "There's beauty in the diversity of experiences."

"But I didn't spend a lot of time wearing girl's clothing or playing with my sister's dolls," I said. I wanted to continue, but I couldn't get words out of my mouth. Shifting my body back and forth to regain my composure, I felt the first tears I had shed since my childhood nearly fifty years earlier hit the pink corduroy pants I was wearing. Then, facing down, I watched the drops fall from my face and splatter, filling the ridges of my pants.

This is what crying is like, I mused.

It was everything: Reliving the decades of self-torment and having compassion for myself. A burgeoning gratitude for discovering who I was. Confusion at the freshness of all my new experiences. Given how deep and long the agony had been, I had, by necessity, developed the ability to bifurcate myself into both an observer and a perpetuator of the injurious actions. The room was completely silent. To divert my discomfort, I looked up at the clock behind Michele.

I opened my mouth but what came out didn't sound like it came from me. "Damn female hormones," I joked, making me laugh and cry some more. I allowed my feelings to wash over me in surges, something I hadn't been capable of for a very long time. At first it was uncomfortable and unfamiliar, but then I let my misgivings vaporize.

"It's so much like I was blocked from accessing this until I got sober and started working a real recovery," I whispered, my voice slightly raspy from crying. Michele was fluent in AA terminology, which helped a lot.

"We are going to go back and look at your history through a female lens," she said, filling me with great comfort. "I think that will be important."

I explained that what I did know is that I detested everything masculine about myself—my penis, chest hair and everything else that came with being a man. Additionally, I seemed to have been surrounded by weak alcoholic men all my life and I naturally gravitated toward the women around me, except for my mother, of course. I groped for the right word because it was more than just being attracted to women.

I suddenly exclaimed, "I've always had an affinity for women."

The room was silent again, but I was not uncomfortable

anymore. My history was important but, at this moment, it only mattered where I was now and that was about as good a place as I had been my entire life. I realized that being present and happy had been almost as rare for me as crying.

I then mentioned I had just been to Mount Sinai Hospital and had my first shot of female hormones. "I have to wait another ten months or so, but I am seriously thinking of getting bottom surgery," I announced.

"My, between your appearance and that, you seem to be moving very fast," she said, a little too sternly, I thought.

"Too fast?" I asked in a childlike way. Before she answered, I did. "I've been baffled all my life and now I know what I want to do. It's not too fast," I declared.

Soon I was telling her I wanted to come out at work, then my plans for coming out at work and eventually the experience itself and its aftermath.

* * *

I had never been a big user of LinkedIn, but I did have a half-baked profile. Occasionally, headhunters reached out to me about job opportunities. Once the *New York Times* story came out, I was flooded with messages from people who wanted to follow me. Among the throng, in the first week, a half dozen transgender people from around the U.S. and Canada reached out to tell me they had found my story inspiring and wanted to chat about their situation.

"I can't tell you when to come out," I told one trans girl who was living in the completely vexing situation of feeling she had to choose between her marriage or coming out.

"My wife lets me play around with my appearance in private but would divorce me if I went public," she bemoaned at the start of our telephone conversation.

"That's a real tough one," I answered. "I was divorced by the time I came out and have no idea if my wife would have stuck with me."

The phone conversation went silent. My new trans friend sighed.

"Just take it slow. You don't have to decide anything today," I said, trying to project some of the self-confidence I had gained. "Keep doing what's right for you and you'll know what to do when the time is right."

Self-doubt hadn't completely left me.

When the time is right? Had I really progressed enough in recovery and self-discovery to know when the time *is* right? Did a year and a half sober after four decades of drinking really qualify me to make such a statement?

DRY DRUNK

1992

THE TWO YEARS I SPENT IN **D.C.** with Michi and Myla when
we left Japan in 1991 were unhappy and tumultuous. Life
worsened, but because it was gradual, I didn't recognize it for
what it was.

I had persuaded a twenty-two-year-old Japanese woman
who had never been outside her country to move with me to
the U.S. and I had no appreciation how difficult the experience was for Michi. Trying in vain to sober up from all the
drinking I did on the flight from Tokyo, I was the recipient of
a torrent of anger from my wife upon our arrival at Dulles.

Michi raged in Japanese, "I'm not going through customs
with you." We had just disembarked, and the other passengers
were staring at us as they purposefully walked by. Dazed after
the prolonged flight from Asia, they shot cursory looks toward
us but quickly turned their attention back to their exhaustion.

"Don't say that. Let's go," I pleaded. I tried grabbing all
the luggage, figuring she'd follow if I had everything and was

headed toward the exit. Announcement after announcement for plane departures blared in the background in English, Japanese and Korean, irritating me still further.

Michi stood her ground, probably starting to realize that she had no plan if she didn't exit the airport with me. Myla, unsteady on her feet after the long flight, just looked back and forth at us not knowing what was going on but instinctively sensing it wasn't good.

'I can't live with someone like you who doesn't care about us," Michi continued. This confused me, because on a deep level I did care, though to her it seemed I did not outwardly manifest compassion, which I probably didn't.

I started to think I might not be able to talk my way out of it. The whole plane had emptied. Even the wheelchair passengers had just rolled past us and we were alone at the gate. I was struck by how antiseptic and sad airports are when empty. I decided to give it one more try.

"Why don't you come through, spend the night and if you still want to go back tomorrow, I'll arrange it," I said calmly, cloaking my anxiety.

Michi paused, looked at Myla for a whole minute, and then nodded so slightly I almost missed it.

She seemed to accept our move to the U.S. once we left the airport, or at least she showed no signs that she didn't. We settled in Falls Church, a tony Virginia suburb of D.C., and I commuted by bike along a sometimes crowded, meandering trail to The National Press Club, where Knight-Ridder Financial had its offices.

Almost immediately, Michi and I grew further and further apart. Cold plates of pasta and curry rice awaited at the end of my day to be heated and eaten alone. Myla and Michi were watching TV or playing together whenever I returned home and only Myla interrupted her activity to raise herself off the floor to greet me.

Michi began spending blocks of time with a Vietnamese artist while I was away at work. On election day, I came home uncharacteristically early to find her in our home with a hapless friend of mine from Japan, Brian, who fancied himself a 1990s hippie.

To be honest, I considered this a desirable outcome as the relationship had already deteriorated into criticism, resentment and alienation. Now I could blame its end on Michi. I was too much of a coward to do anything to make it better or find a dignified way out.

Myla, Brian and Michi moved up to New York. The day they left included one of those moments when the detail of the event is forever engraved in my consciousness, never to be diminished no matter how much time passes.

Before heading out, Michi hugged me and said, "I'm sorry it has to be this way." She then began heading down the steps of our second-floor apartment. She ordered, "We're leaving now. Come on Myla."

"I don't want to leave Daddy," she replied hugging my legs as if she drew her life force from them. "Come with us, Daddy!"

"I can't honey. I have to stay here to work," I lied.

Myla's wail echoed up the staircase for what seemed an eternity. For months afterward, I heard the same squeals and sometimes had a hard time believing they were not real.

I pulled a half-gallon of rum from the cabinet above the sink, pouring and drinking three large rum and cokes in rapid succession. From there, my nightly imbibing, never moderate to begin with, doubled and sometimes tripled. I came to see D.C. as soulless and preoccupied with only one thing, politics. I always had a hard time divorcing places where I was unhappy from my feelings about them.

Latching onto a path to New York to be near Myla, I applied and was accepted to the prestigious Knight-Bagehot

Fellowship for journalists at Columbia University. I bid good riddance to D.C.

After my year of study at Columbia in Upper Manhattan, I returned to Knight-Ridder but in New York. My career took off, mainly because the person who had run our Asian operations, a boyish Brit named Paul Lowe, was made the global head of Editorial. He took no time in installing the people he had previously worked with and trusted in positions of authority in the U.S.

My return to Knight-Ridder also meant I encountered Jackie, who I had met briefly before in Tokyo when she was checking it out as a possible new work location. Jackie was a senior copy editor at Knight-Ridder and one of the few who, if she got her hands on your copy, was going to render it appreciably better. We became fast friends and part of a circle of reporters and editors who went out drinking in the bars on the first floor of the World Financial Center after work several nights a week.

The simple camaraderie part changed one night at a journalist company retreat in Tarrytown, a Hudson River city within easy commuting distance of Manhattan. A bunch of us reporters and editors were in her hotel room raiding the mini bar and joking around when it was suddenly just the two of us.

Somebody had put *The Karate Kid* on the TV in the background. The part of the movie was playing where the main character does "the crane," standing on one leg and coiling the other with arms outstretched on either side of the body.

We giggled and one of us suggested having a competition to see who could do the crane the longest. She tried first but, suffused with alcohol, couldn't stay on one leg for more than ten seconds. Swaying back and forth, her raised leg fell with a thud.

"I told you; you wouldn't be able to do it,' I said, enjoying teasing her. The movie moved on, but we didn't.

"Let's see you try," she said, daring me. She took a sip of the gin and tonic she had mixed from the mini bar and turned back to see my attempt.

I went down in half the time she did.

"Ha, I win," she threw back at me, holding up her arms in victory and picking up her drink and downing the rest. I pulled a miniature bottle of Bacardi out of the mini bar and fixed myself a fresh drink.

"Not so fast. Here's the final challenge," I shot back, challenging her. "Same time, whoever's up leg touches first, loses."

The overhead lights saturated the room with brightness, highlighting all the small stains and pieces of trash that cleaning had failed to remove. It could have been any hour of the night.

"Not fair. I already won," she said, feigning disgust with the competition, but I could see I had her hooked.

We said go at the same time and brought up our legs. Simultaneously growing wobbly, our risen legs came crashing down in front of us and tipsy as we were, we stumbled for a bit before regaining our balance. We ended up facing each other, our flushed cheeks not three feet away. As Jackie was righting herself, I looked into the brown spheres of her eyes and put my lips on hers. She didn't completely back away but broke it off soon.

Quickly regaining her composure, she straightened her blouse and pants. She brought her arm to her mouth, unconsciously wiping the kiss off her lips. It was time to restore British decorum. "It's late and we ought to be getting to bed," she said stiffly.

I said good night and left. We didn't have a chance to talk the next morning, but in the afternoon, she said she'd need to think over what happened. Sunday night she called me and suggested we go on a date.

At the outset, dating meant just going out in our work circle of friends and pretending that nothing had changed. Then I started staying over, walking from my shared apartment on West End Avenue to hers near the park on West 85th Street. Having partied with me for a year now, Jackie must have known I liked my booze, but she didn't know to what extent I needed it.

I would drink a half pint of rum on my way over and have some miniatures tucked in my bag for good measure if needed. At her apartment, we usually split a bottle of wine between us, and I tried to be just woozy enough where the wine became maintenance for my buzz.

About a year later, I proposed to her in a quaint little town up the Hudson River called Cold Spring and we were married at New York City Hall, with Myla present as the witness. Since we both had been married before, we decided to keep it low key. The three of us went out for a nice sushi lunch afterwards.

Jackie provided me with a comfort I hadn't felt in years. She was stable, kind, a good listener, and intuitive. Being around her helped me keep my demons at bay some of the time. Unfortunately, over time, I took all her exceptional qualities for granted.

Jackie gave birth to our first son Liam in 2001 after some difficulty conceiving, which turned out to be the result of my body's tendency to kill off most of my sperm. I was later diagnosed with varicose veins in my scrotum, which warmed the sack to an inhospitable temperature for the sperm. This was yet another sign that my manhood did not wear well.

After seeing how much I drank every day, encouraging me to cut down, and then watching me fail in restaurant experiments we devised to limit my drinking, Jackie had already had enough and demanded I get help. I sought assistance for the first time for my drinking, attending outpatient counseling at Smithers, a prominent alcohol and substance abuse center at the base of Central Park.

With the aid of that program, I was somehow able to stay sober for almost three years. I had tried and rejected Alcoholics Anonymous as something that didn't suit me. As a result, I had no ongoing support, but I didn't think I needed any. It would be a long time before I understood that willpower alone is not a recipe for sustained sobriety.

We purchased an apartment at 103rd Street and Central Park West, catching the area, which traditionally had been viewed as too far uptown, just as it was gentrifying. But then disaster struck New York in the form of Sept. 11, 2001. The offices of Knight-Ridder Financial, now called Bridge News, were right across the street from the Twin Towers.

Jackie, Liam, and I had just returned from a week in Block Island, Rhode Island, and the day dawned clear and crisp. Surveying the wreckage from right across the street, I left our building, and started walking uptown. It turns out I lost my job that day as the news operation I worked for was soon shuttered.

I had no employment, a one-year-old and a now undesirable apartment in New York City, which in an instant became a place nobody really wanted to live in anymore. We decided to leave—for Westchester—partly to be close to my daughter. Brian, Michi, and Lane, their new son, had moved out of the city into a working-class Hudson River enclave of Dobbs Ferry.

As a trial, we moved for a year to North Salem, which was on the outer fringes of Westchester and a New York horse country epicenter. We rented a small house, which had a horse and stable, settling in for a bitter winter followed by a spring that kicked up the worst of Jackie's plant allergies.

This was the first time in my adult life without work and I often despaired that I might never find another, leaving my family destitute. But in May of 2002, Merrill Lynch offered me a job in lower Manhattan in a building right next to the one from where I had witnessed the 9/11 catastrophe.

THE DIRTY RIDGE

2003

JACKIE HAD BEEN SCOURING northern Westchester for a place to settle and found a very reasonably priced home in a town called Pound Ridge, the triangular part of Westchester that juts into Fairfield County, Connecticut.

I resided in that house for 14 years, the longest I have ever lived in the same place, but by the time I left I branded it as evil, just as Rehoboth, Nishi Funabashi and Washington D.C. had received the Devil's stamp. For most of my life I believed that I was a unique recipient of misfortune, but particularly in the form of the places I had lived.

Once I finally made my way into AA and listened to what was being said, I realized that if nearly every place I had lived was malevolent, then I was the common denominator, and therefore, likely the problem.

In early spring, Jackie and I walked the property before making an offer for the house. We were surrounded by denuded trees, swampy wetlands and a rocky ridgeline with moss and ferns sprouting out of its crevices. It was much colder than I remember spring being when I was younger. Perhaps the fact I was now 41 had something to do with that.

The brown and orange house was an A-frame with a flat, one-story wing grafted on to it. It had an air of having been abandoned for a while.

"Is this really the best we can do?" I wondered out loud. Though I had worked at Merrill Lynch for less than a year, I already was becoming pampered and thought I deserved better.

We were standing in the backyard, which clearly only existed because somebody had illegally filled in wetlands. There was an in-ground pool, but it had not been used in years and thick weeds grew up around it, greedily asserting that the pool area belonged to them.

"You have to look at the potential," Jackie said, thrusting her hands into the recently waxed Barbour jacket, which she always proclaimed would last her until the day she died. "We are getting into this skyrocketing real estate market at a very attractive place."

"But it is going to take so much work," I moaned, picking up some acorns and tossing them into the nearby swamp.

The weak sun made no effort to hold back the wind cavorting around the property, stirring up mischief. Tree branches knocked against each other, and long dead, brittle brown leaves leapt, seemingly enlivened again. A sudden gust drew my attention to buildings just across our property line.

"We also don't have a lot of privacy," I said, continuing my fault finding without offering any other alternative.

"We can make this work," Jackie affirmed, turning her back on me and walking away. She was done hearing my complaints and had already made up her mind to buy the place.

Relatively vast geographically, Pound Ridge is home to only 6,000 residents. It's not a desirable commuter location to New York City because there are no train stations nearby.

This helped to keep the population low. As opposed to the wide-open fields of horse country in nearby Bedford and North Salem, Pound Ridge possesses miles of rocky ridges, hills and very little in the way of fields. It is a nightmare during electrical storms as trees with shallow root systems topple, and, in fits of selfishness, spitefully pull down power lines.

The old town center is filled with grand colonial white houses, but the town's history is modest. The local artisans were basket makers for, among other things, the valuable Norwalk oysters that were harvested in nearby Long Island Sound.

For most of my time there, Pound Ridge was a verdant place I enjoyed on weekends but an obstacle to be navigated during the week over the course of a two-hour commute each way by car, train, and subway to my office in lower Manhattan.

I began that commute to Merrill Lynch from North Salem and did it for the next 15 years from Pound Ridge. The trip back and forth to lower Manhattan snatched my soul to the extent I still had one, which by then I doubted. I would either catch the first local at 4:45 a.m. or first express shortly after five. Given the 30-minute drive to the station, and the need to pump coffee in me at that absurd hour, I rose from bed before four a.m. Once I arrived in the city, I'd take the subway downtown to Merrill and then Goldman, tacking on another thirty minutes. To get from work to home, I had to do the same in reverse, except it was worse because I didn't feel like reading, answering my emails or doing anything remotely constructive. I mainly wanted to sleep.

In terms of the job itself, I was fortunate that at Merrill I had a kind, experienced manager in Jessica Oppenheim. I began at Merrill knowing nothing about media relations and Jessica allowed me to handle news stories of consequence for the Global Markets and Investment Banking division, which included sales and trading and investment banking. During my time at Merrill, I picked up the basics of media relations and turned out to have a talent for it. Having been a financial reporter for 15 years, I knew a lot about markets, and though I considered myself a social misfit, I understood how to talk to journalists and make them feel comfortable.

It had been a strange time to be at Merrill as its new leader Stan O'Neill was just taking the reins and was installing allies across the firm. Retirements and restructurings were happening left and right. One thing I noticed during my time at Merrill was that its executives were obsessed with Goldman Sachs. Part of my responsibilities included a weekly media report on both Merrill Lynch and competitors. The clips everybody wanted to see were ones about Goldman Sachs. What dumbfounded me was that no matter how much Goldman messed up, it never seemed to get any bad press.

HOT WAX

2004

In the summer, I was approached by a Goldman recruiter to interview for a media relations position to cover Fixed Income, Currencies and Commodities, Goldman's famed commodities and bond trading juggernaut. After a dozen or so interviews during the summer, I took off with my family for vacation.

With limited cell coverage, I was standing in the parking lot of Misquamicut Beach in Rhode Island on an overcast day with sea spray jumping over the dunes to gently baptize me. Peter Rose, a gregarious Kiwi who was beloved by journalists and reveled in daily catnaps at his desk, called to give me the good news that Goldman was extending me an offer.

The first few years I worked at Goldman, I was certainly busy, but I didn't really sink my teeth into any issues that were particularly memorable. Goldman was practically minting money and shook off virtually any whiff of scandal. I developed bonds with the senior leaders in the division who were generous with their time whenever I asked but seemed to regard me as an afterthought.

Early in my Goldman tenure, I began drinking again. There was no catalyst, but rather once I stopped, I never resolved to stay stopped. I was merely taking a hiatus to get the drinking monster on a tight leash which I could use to make it heel when it threatened to uncontrollably lunge. At the outset, I didn't buy bottles of liquor, but rather I pounded two quick cocktails at Grand Central. This construct was unsatisfying: New York City bar drinks are not cheap, and they never seemed to come fast enough, which annoyed me when I was trying to catch specific trains.

Eventually I started buying half pints just outside of Goldman Sachs' then-headquarters in lower Manhattan on Broad Street, with the stern promise to myself that I would never drink once I got home. It soon became extremely unpleasant waking up from a quick nap on the train after drinking knowing that I would not be able to imbibe for the rest of the night. For the longest time, I held out on bringing liquor back into the house, but at one point, I could not resist and once that genie was out of the bottle, I began my slow and inevitable slide toward disaster.

What should have been a warning sign was a week in late 2004 when Jackie was away with Liam in the UK. I had my first multi-day continuous binge, which deeply frightened me but clearly not enough. I know the time of year because, for some reason, I had just gotten a Michael McDonald CD, *In the Spirit: A Christmas Album.* The whole week, I never bothered changing the CD and that album played endlessly.

On day three of my binge, I called in sick to work saying I had a stomach virus. Drinking around the clock for a week, I woke up, swigged, fell asleep and repeated. With no food in my stomach, I detoxed myself two days before Jackie came home. Craving sleep, I could not get any rest. Then there was sweating, followed by chills, which sent my body into spasms.

Hands quivering, stomach shut to everything but alcohol, and alternatively freezing and roasting, I slept for an hour or so the night before Jackie returned, woke up and started cleaning the sheets again, which were soaked and smelled like rum-soaked urine. Several hours before Jackie was due home, I couldn't hold out any longer and downed a half a pint of rum followed by a nap, which is where Jackie found me.

She barged into the bedroom. "There's no food in the refrigerator. We just traveled all this way, and you couldn't be bothered to go to the store once!"

"I've had a stomach virus," I shot back. I'd told myself that lie so many times I had begun to believe it. It certainly was true that my stomach hurt.

"I know you've been drinking again," Jackie said calmly, clearly seething beneath the surface.

"Just a little," I replied. This is what I always said when I'd been caught.

"I think you need some help again." She was less understanding than she was the first time around.

* * *

Jackie always gave the most thoughtful Christmas and birthday presents, even to me, despite my derelictions. One such gift revived a long-dormant fragment within me.

By 2005, our family was taking summer vacations every year to either Block Island or Cape Cod. I had never abandoned detesting everything male about myself or avoiding looking at myself in the mirror; one of the most blatantly visible insults was the thick hair on my chest and back. If I dwelt upon it, I would get angry and berate the universe for saddling me with such a noxious physical trait.

Jackie was aware of this antipathy and in the summer

brought out electric clippers to shear me like a lamb. The thick layer of course black hair (with some white sprinkled in) would gather at my feet to be carried by the wind to who knows where. One year for my birthday, she surprised me with a gift certificate for waxing at the hair salon she frequented in Pound Ridge.

I entered with the trepidation of the unknown. The clinician directed me to take my shirt off and get relaxed on the treatment bed as she heated the wax. It felt hot, but strangely comforting as she troweled it onto my body, but any peace I experienced was disrupted when she pulled the first giant tuft up. The skin on my stomach turned a fiery, angry red immediately and began throbbing. This particular clinician didn't seem to be especially experienced, and she took two full hours to do my whole torso, sometimes returning to spots that had already been done because the hair had not been completely removed. Fortunately, several weeks later, she was replaced by Helen, who was skilled and could do the whole job in a humane 30 minutes.

As much as the whole exercise pained me, the sensation of my shirt catching on my raw skin and not sliding easily over my matted chest hair revitalized me, albeit for a woefully short spell. The hairless consciousness lasted about a week but then stubble sprouted just like it had when the thunderbolt had been carved into my chest hair 20 years earlier. The itchiness from sweating reminded me of the Tokyo dance floors I had frequented. My present life in Pound Ridge seemed universes away from that time.

TEFLON NO MORE

2007

THE NATURE OF MY JOB AT GOLDMAN began to change in 2007 with the start of the financial crisis, though at the time nobody foresaw how dire events would become. I was not yet at the place in my career where people thought to post me when something behind the scenes was going on that might suddenly burst into an external press issue.

Certain bond markets started to take bad turns in 2007 but those cracks in the system were not visible to the person in the street. And, so three years into my tenure at Goldman, I finally got to immerse myself in a story that really mattered.

I picked up my phone and barked my standard greeting, "Michael speaking." I'd refined my tone to give off the vibe that I was wary of anybody calling me. That tended to disorient people, who expected something friendlier. If I knew them, I would immediately become sociable. This routine, which all happened in a split second, suited my people philosophy—being distrustful of everybody who called until I could ascertain whether I could relax and be comfortable with them.

In late 2007 into 2008, reporters began bombarding us with questions about the carnage of the mortgage-backed securities markets and how one of our trading desks had made a lot of money—about $4 billion—shorting that market or positioning itself to benefit if prices went down.

"I was talking to somebody, and he said if I really want to highlight the winners from the volatility in the mortgage market, I ought to take a look at your mortgage trading desk," one veteran reporter said to me over the phone, effectively throwing down the gauntlet.

I was sitting in my cramped office at 85 Broad Street on a low floor that only received direct beams of light through its narrow windows at rare times of year. It was mid-winter with murky overcast skies, extinguishing for the moment any chance the sun would smile on me.

I let her go on. It was important to get as much information about what she had.

"Your desk, the structured product trading desk, thought the housing market would crater," she explained, adding, "They were right, and made a lot of money."

I knew about the trading activity she was talking about, so I decided to push back a little bit when I had the opportunity. On complex stories like this one, reporter interactions with public relation types like me, flacks as we are sometimes referred to, could be multi-week skirmishes with each side adhering to unspoken rules involving trust and honesty. If one side was caught violating these tenets, the whole interaction became poisoned, making it impossible to have good faith interactions.

I muttered a "mmh" to let her know I was listening but chose not to respond yet.

"They were placing a huge bet that housing prices would fall," she said, growing increasingly excited as she built to the end of her spiel.

"I don't think it really was a bet. We had long mortgage positions and needed to hedge them," I responded, breaking my silence. This was a line I repeated dozens of times to dozens of reporters. Journalists loved to portray Wall Street as a giant casino with investment banks placing wagers, which could have a big payout or loss. Nobody at Goldman Sachs liked the word "bet" but reporters adored it and we had only limited success at getting them to keep it out of their stories.

"Well, the result was the same—you made a lot of money," the reporter answered back, raising her voice a little. Reporters didn't like it when they thought flacks were playing semantics. They wrote the stories and made the decisions about what words to use. We had to be careful to make suggestions, not demands.

"It's different because we lost money on some positions, and our hedges offset those losses," I explained. Sometimes the reporter and flack were saying the same things, but the friction was over the words chosen.

A narrow slice of sunlight, which had snuck through two tall buildings several hundred feet from mine, hit my chest. If it had been a laser, it would have ripped me in two.

"I don't know why you're so worried," she said, backing off from our verbal jousting. "You made a lot of money. Isn't that good?"

Despite my efforts to stifle it, I sighed and then went silent. Reporters often said this to me, not knowing that there were dozens of ways a story could appear positive on the surface but end up being a huge internal headache, particularly if it alienated clients or regulators.

"I wouldn't be so sure of that," I responded. The conversation ended for the day, but it would continue. And, this story would morph from "Goldman Sachs made a boatload of money shorting the market" to "Goldman Sachs kept selling mortgage products to its clients at the same time it was betting the market was going down."

The "Big Short" stories were certainly not the last to challenge Goldman Sachs' reputation. The office of Corporate Communications was in crisis mode for the next six years.

Under the watchful eye of my new boss, Lucas van Praag, an erudite Brit with a wicked sense of humor, I also handled the call one late Friday afternoon from *Rolling Stone* freelancer Matt Taibbi who ended up comparing Goldman Sachs to a vampire squid, a metaphor that still clings over a decade later.

Lucas made the right decision in not gracing the story with a comment but couldn't help himself when other media outlets followed up on Monday with requests for comment on the story. Jumping in with colorful, hyperbolic language, he ensured our response was going to be part of the news cycle.

One of his retorts: "[Taibbi's] story is an hysterical compilation of conspiracy theories. Notable ones missing are Goldman Sachs as the third shooter [in John F. Kennedy's assassination] and faking the first lunar landing."

* * *

While markets gyrated and Goldman was under relentless public criticism for the financial crisis, I was suffering my own crisis. By this time, I was buying quart bottles of rum or vodka, drinking all the way home, sobering up for a bit, only to resume my drinking after dinner. I was constantly in search of ways to be buzzed but to appear sober, a seemingly paradoxical state but one which I relentlessly pursued for decades.

One of my favorite sobering-up strategies was to open our home's swimming pool as early as possible in the year and keep it open as late as possible. Although the frigid waters in May and September gave me headaches and pilfered my breath, I concluded (deluding myself of course) that I was walking into the house stone cold sober.

I was also starting to drink midday on Saturday or Sunday. There was a liquor store close to our house that was open 363 days a year. If I ran out of liquor on Saturday, I would be there at 11:55 a.m. along with another half dozen degenerate drunks on Sunday to get my stash for the day when it opened at noon.

After going to bed one Sunday, I awoke in the middle of the night with a deep and pervasive despair that my drinking and the neglect of my family was leading me toward oblivion and ruin. I had a pint of rum left in my stone wall stash and I gathered it up in the darkness at 4:25 a.m. and headed to catch my train.

When I arrived at Stamford Station, I turned the engine off and sat silently in the car. It seemed like an eternity and at first, I did not consciously know why I had not gotten out of the car, but I realized I was weighing the pros and cons of taking a drink then. Lights illuminated the station in the distance, but it was quiet and dark in the parking garage. I knew myself and there was a good chance I would finish the whole pint and sneak out of work to buy more. The depth of my self-hatred made the idea of even fleeting relief appealing. I drank before work for the first time.

I did this sporadically over the next few months, sneaking out to bars at noon or to buy nips from nearby liquor stores. Of course, several of my co-workers noticed and in the most benevolent way imaginable, they pulled me aside.

"Are you okay?" one kind person in our group asked me when I was on my way out of work that day.

"I'm fine. Why do you ask?" I said nonchalantly, though a plume of bile shot up from my stomach, burning the sides of my throat.

"You've not really been yourself," she said narrowing her eyes and tightening up her whole body in discomfort. "It's not really my business but it seems like sometimes you're not up to doing your job. Is there anything I can do?"

"Nope. I'm good," I shot back. I just wanted her out of the office. I had deceived myself into believing that nobody knew about my drinking and here was proof that I was wrong.

"Well, I think you should probably get some help," she said, ending the conversation and leaving the office for the weekend.

Shortly thereafter, I called the now familiar employee assistance hotline and set up a meeting with one of the counselors, where I agreed to go back to outpatient and give AA a try again. I didn't work a great program of recovery, but I tried more than I had in the past, getting myself to meetings in the city at 6:30 a.m. Staying sober six months was an accomplishment at this stage of my drinking career but toward the end, I was told I needed to go to London for a couple of weeks to help the local team. I just loved drinking in London, and I knew it was going to be impossible not to.

Despite the severity of my drinking at the time, I was able to maintain a high degree of energy and enthusiasm for my work and on the strength of my efforts handling all the challenging stories about Goldman Sachs in 2008 and 2009, I was named a managing director in 2010.

Though one notch shy of partner, achieving this title was notable. I received the news while working in the London office and went out to lunch to celebrate with one of my co-workers at a pub. A painting of a giant white swan both lorded over the establishment and gave the pub its name. As I stared at the bird in disgust, I had no reason to believe my drinking would interfere with the progression of my career at Goldman.

No reason at all.

THERE'S NO PLACE
LIKE HOME

2012

BY THIS TIME, JACKIE AND I had our second son, Connor. Through the years, I did the best I could to show love to my boys: We'd enjoy throwing a football around, playing board games, reading books, and hanging out at the playground. On one level, I was running from my father but, as long as I kept drinking, I was being pulled back toward an alcoholic whirlpool and the morass of weak, drunken men who were abundant on both sides of my family.

When I was growing up, there had been no men around me whom I aspired to be like. I yearned to be a good father, but I didn't know how. If only I had known how to take the male gender out of parenthood, perhaps I could have settled into a more comfortable role preparing the boys for the outside world. I didn't want them to venture into the world metaphorically naked and lobotomized like me.

* * *

My mother sometimes took the train down to New York to visit us for a long weekend. After I collected Myla from Dobbs Ferry, we all went on deep forest hikes in the spring or apple-picking sojourns in the fall.

A couple of months after one of my mother's spring visits, we were up in Rehoboth sitting on a screened-in back porch my brother John had built at my parent's house, the one I had grown up in. My father was drunk and so was my mother. Whenever she had too much wine, she became quite aggressive.

The porch was a jewel and allowed us to be outdoors during cooler summer evenings. Normally, outside was off limits because the swamp that encircled the property was a prolific breeding ground for mosquitos engaged in fierce competition with each other to find exposed, sweaty flesh. We reminisced about my mother's most recent trip to Pound Ridge. Everybody except me, who was still a vegetarian, liked salmon and I usually splurged for wild salmon even though it could run 35 dollars a pound. It was out of season when she visited our home, so I had served everybody some high-quality New Zealand farm-raised salmon at 20 bucks a pound.

My father, on the cusp of becoming unable to put together a meal, fried cod for everybody that night in Rehoboth and at least this time, it was neither charred nor semi raw.

We had a table on the porch, and my parents, Jackie and my children sat down for what promised to be a tasty dinner. The wine had been poured, the food was on plates, and we had just picked up our utensils, ready to feast.

"This is certainly better than that crap you served when I was at your house," my mother suddenly blurted out. She addressed me in a slurred voice but refused to make eye contact. Her gaze was fixed on the backyard where the moon illuminated the puddingstones, which poked up through the ground like mushrooms on the forest floor.

"What are you talking about—that was good salmon," I said, defending myself as I rocked back and forth on a wooden swing I liked. I found it calming whenever my family tried to wind me up.

"It was that disgusting, disgusting farm-raised salmon. They swim and eat their own crap," she said twisting up her face as she did when she wanted to make an emphatic point.

"Mom, that was good salmon," I answered, realizing as the words left my mouth that it was better to shut up, depriving her diatribe of the fuel it needed to continue.

"Maybe for you. I will never eat that disgusting crap again. It's sickening," she continued relentlessly. As she talked, she poked at her cod as if deciding whether it, too, was disgusting and sickening.

I was unable to restrain myself. "Well, I didn't see anything left on your plate." I had had a little bit too much wine myself, deterring me from what should have been my primary focus—ending the conversation.

Everybody else, heads bowed, silently raised forkful after forkful of cod, baked potatoes and peas to their mouth. This conversation was a losing proposition and everybody but me recognized that.

We both paused and looked outside at the throbbing green and yellow dots in the air as male fireflies sought to attract females with lengthy and intense pulses.

"I only ate it to be polite. It nearly made me sick," she repeated herself.

There was nothing more to say. Her vitriol sent me to the yellow kitchen counter to drench her bitter voice in my head with Bacardi dark rum. It was no consolation of mine that in my mother's waning years of her life, the only fish she ate—sardines, salmon, or tuna—came out of a can.

* * *

On another occasion, I was hanging out in the "cranberry room," the bedroom in my parents' new house painted in the color of Massachusetts' favorite berry. Having some time on my hands, I decided to explore the cedar room, a large walk-in closet my mother had had built to store her vast clothes collection. Apparently, cedar absorbs moisture, providing an extra layer of protection for valuable dresses and blouses.

The room contained thousands of dollars of fancy dresses, crazy Halloween outfits and boxes of shoes. On the far wall, showcased by area lighting, my mother's costume jewelry was arrayed on glass shelves. I came into the cedar room to forage from time to time, banking that my mother's compulsive hoarding of items might supply me with something I needed but hadn't wanted to pay for.

On one of the shelves, I found ten pairs of winter gloves and three brand new belts. I took one of each but decided to take a pass on the five Star Wars Lego sets that had never been opened.

I wouldn't say my mother ever kept a clean house but at least the viewable areas appeared to be tidy. The same could not be said for the hidden nooks and crannies of the house. There was a large pile of dresses in tangled knots covering the floor, with dozens of boxes of unopened shoes poking out of the mound.

I was about to leave with my gloves and belt when a pink sweater that was obviously from Ireland caught my eye. Beautifully knitted, with a label that read, "Carraig Donn," its front was lined with black and brown wooden buttons. Though I had avoided pink all my life, in this moment I could not understand my aversion to the color.

After slipping it on and doing up the buttons, I stilled myself. Nothing in me rebelled, so I resolved to take it. But first I sniffed it and was immediately hit by a combination of cedar and old cardboard. After all, it was probably born about the same time I was. A good dry cleaning in New York would certainly do the trick.

Continuing to go through the hanging items, I pushed the sparkly gowns out of the way and got to the pants section. Everything was a size 2 or 4 which meant nothing to me at the time, though everything seemed a bit small. My mother had been at her most extravagant in in her late forties and early fifties and had lost so much weight from compulsive aerobics, we siblings wondered if she had some kind of eating disorder.

The black leather pants I selected were sleek and unblemished (at most they had been worn a couple of times). I slid my shoes off, slipped my legs in and bit by bit, shimmied them up my legs. The waist button wouldn't fit into its hole, but it was close. If I started running more, maybe I could get them to fit. Looking down, I conjured the specter of myself preparing for a night out in Roppongi.

Where had I gone?

* * *

Shortly after my shopping expedition in the cedar room, I was summoned back to Massachusetts, as my father was in hospice and near death. His demise had been steady, alcoholically sad, and pathetic. He had fallen down the stairs in his home, blaming it on a dog, and broken his hip. Never an active man, he put off doing rehab for as long as possible. He suffered a series of other physical problems that required hospitalizations, but since he always resumed drinking upon discharge, he had to be detoxed every time something new cropped up.

My mother set him up in a separate room on the first floor of the new house they had bought. The moving was another event that set him off because for as long as I can remember, whenever my mother threatened to move, he'd say, "My next move will be up the road," meaning the town cemetery. He would urinate all over himself and regularly spit up blood.

When the end was near, he was put into an urgent care facility in Providence. I was home the week he died and watched as he sipped thickened orange soda through a straw.

When I entered the room for the first time, he rasped to my mother, "If Michael is here, I really must be dying."

This emaciated man reeking of death had loomed large in my consciousness all my life, mostly in a not so positive way. As I sat on the edge of his bed and watched him drinking that orange soda, I let go all the resentments I had toward him and saw him for the provider he was to the family and the battered son of the bitter woman who was his mother.

I eulogized him at his wake and said some words at his grave. Good thing I did, because no one else in my family stepped forward to share that responsibility with me, leaving me resentful and sad at the same time.

"Dad, you always said you looked forward to dying because you'd just get to sleep. Sleep well," I said and tossed his favorite tam-o-shanter into his grave and walked away. Of course, we had a bag piper play, "Amazing Grace."

BLIZZARDS OF BOOZE

2013

I WAS DRINKING HEAVILY, and my marriage was fraying before my eyes, though I tried to block it out as much as possible. Jackie didn't confront me about my drinking unless I was totally sloppy, especially in front of the boys. If I was not challenged, I assumed I was getting away with it and that I had a license to drink more.

I had been drinking off and on for 35 years. I slept at most three hours a night, awakening to the overpowering desire to be dead. I either fantasized for the next two or three hours about ways to kill myself or slipped downstairs to find a hidden bottle to swig from, which sometimes bought me a couple more hours of erratic sleep.

I continued to pursue my quixotic quest to find a way to drink without consequences—no afternoon naps, no slurring, no hangovers and no suicidal ideations. When I picked up alcohol again in London after not drinking for a half year, there was a ferocity that was not there before. I had stopped doing all the daily things we must do in recovery—going to AA meetings, praying, calling, and helping others. Now that I was naked and defenseless against the first drink, I ran towards it, oblivious to the consequences, which I knew well by now.

When I lost control, I abandoned all restraint. This was especially true of business trips. In the hearts of most alcoholics is a special fondness for flying. Perhaps like Halloween, it is the anonymity or the fact that (until recently) once airborne, passengers are unreachable and therefore shed, at least temporarily, all responsibility. For me, business travel overseas brought only peril.

On one such quick trip to Canada, I finished off a half pint of vodka at five in the morning before leaving my house, and by 7:30 a.m., now at La Guardia airport, I was cursing the facility because it did not start selling wine and beer until 8 a.m.

Misfortunate accumulated as I bumped into a former work colleague who also was on his way up to Canada. Samuel had been one of the people who passionately argued in my favor during the managing director selection process the year I was elevated. I was eternally grateful to him but that didn't mean I wanted to talk to him that morning. Drinking in the morning took work: I had to get it just right or when the buzz wore off it felt horrific.

"Michael, Michael, hey...." Samuel nearly had to yell to get my attention.

Finally turning and acknowledging his greeting, I mouthed, "Oh, hi," though I was barely able to hide my distaste at having to engage in conversation. Since our departure gates were adjacent, I had no choice but to sit down next to him. Both areas were bursting with businesspeople guzzling Starbucks and trying to make sure they were current on every last email until takeoff cut their umbilical cord to their co-workers and clients.

Tall, thin, with sandy free-flowing hair, Samuel had left Goldman a couple of years ago for a chief operating officer job at a smaller firm and we hadn't kept in touch.

"How's the new job going?" I asked, at least attempting to be civil and conversational. Everyone around me was so intense it hurt.

"Okay. I fly up to Montreal a couple of times a month," he explained. "I like the people who run the firm so it's working for me," he said, the words pouring out of his mouth. He was British, but anything but reserved.

It would have been natural for me to respond to keep the conversation going but I had just had a mind burp and temporarily lost contact with where I was. Out the window on the runway, planes were maneuvering toward the takeoff queue, leaving dancing clouds of jet fuel visible in the frigid January air.

He picked things up on my behalf. I couldn't be sure if I was imagining it, but his brow began to furrow. "How's it been being the big MD?" he asked, smiling. He clearly recognized he had been the kingmaker. Or was he an inquisitor, knowing something was wrong with me? Paranoia rising like stomach acid, I knew I had to find a way out of this soon.

"You know, it's slowed a bit from the worst during the crisis when you were there, but we're still on heightened alert," I said, proud of my first coherent sentence in the conversation.

"Any more calls from McClatchy?" he asked, referring to a newspaper chain that employed a reporter who gave us fits for several months when writing a series about the mortgage crisis.

"Nope, they're thankfully leaving us alone," I answered, suddenly glancing at my phone. It was 8:01 and wine was being served so I excused myself to go to the bathroom, never returning, which I felt a little guilty about but not enough to do anything about it.

I eagerly purchased two bottles of cheap white wine when the shop opened and then a half hour later a quart of Bacardi Limon Rum at duty free which I began drinking before I even got on the plane, all the time looking over my shoulder to make sure Samuel wasn't watching me. But he had already boarded. I passed out once I got into my seat on the aircraft.

The rest of the trip was a blur. I managed the interviews with senior Canadian executives and local journalists, which was the purpose of the trip. When the day was over, I realized my hotel was down by the lake, which was about a half mile from Goldman's Toronto office. Calling a cab seemed like an almost impossible task so I started walking—in a sudden blizzard. By the time I reached the hotel, my clothes were sodden from the three or four tumbles I had taken on the slick sidewalks.

The next evening, as I settled into my seat for the two-hour flight back from Toronto to New York, I prayed with fervor that God would strike the plane from the sky and end my miserable existence in a ball of flames. The plane did not crash but I was crashing and burning. I decided I was in no shape to go home to Westchester but instead called my wife from the office and said my flight was delayed. She knew I was lying.

* * *

Around this time, our Corporate Communications group decided to have an "offsite." Bankers and traders at investment banks love to hold "offsites" at least once a year to plot out strategic direction. These shindigs were often held during winter in places like Florida or Southern California. Non-revenue producing areas like mine typically could only get budget when times were flush. In my 18 years at Goldman, Corporate Communications had only two offsites. Though we were joined by all my colleagues from other regions of the world, the meetings were held in New York, so they hardly seemed like offsites to me.

Because the global team met so infrequently and we had

so many new people, a couple of my co-workers were planning a game where photos from the distant past would be displayed online, and attendees would have to guess the identity of each person.

My mind sped to my punkish time in Japan, and I knew I had to find a photo of me with a perm, army boots and a leather jacket. Digging through plastic cases in the room over our garage one Saturday afternoon, I soon found the boxes that contained my photo albums, which to my surprise had pink rose covers. Did I do that?

I found the photos I was looking for, removing them carefully because some had begun to stick to the brittle plastic covering that had held them in place all these years. At the bottom of one of the boxes, I spied a little red jewelry case. Shaking as I opened it, the case opened a portal to my past.

In it was my wedding ring from my marriage to Michi, which I eventually gave to Myla as a keepsake; and two thunderbolt earrings that I had bought to complement the thunderbolt shorn into my chest hair. Again, memories of Atchan, the Tokyo discos, and Ni-Chome frolicked before me. For an instant, I was able to put aside the horror movie my life had become. Locating the two holes still visible on my left ear, I quickly pushed the back findings through the layer of membrane that had formed from years of disuse. Maybe they could act as an amulet, restoring some of the joy I had had in Japan.

I felt closer to being whole, but it wouldn't last. Our family's world was about to be upended.

THE PAPAYA

2014

IN APRIL OF 2014, my then eight-year-old son Connor was diagnosed with a Wilms tumor, a type of pediatric tumor that grows out of the kidneys of some young children. We had just noticed that one of the sides of his stomach area was distended, bulging out in a semi-circle. He was on the operating table three days later at Columbia Presbyterian in Upper Manhattan.

The size of a small melon, the tumor had moved his innards into unnatural places, requiring delicate surgery that lasted some seven hours. Jackie and I passed the grim time watching 11 or 12 episodes of *Frasier* on a laptop, the witty humor sometimes helping us forget what was going on in a room not too far from where we were. Misfortune had brought us closer than we had been in a long time.

A nurse slipped into the room every couple of hours and told us that the surgery was more complex than anticipated and was still ongoing.

"Can you tell us anything?" Jackie asked when we saw her head poke out from around a corner.

"The doctors are working hard to remove the tumor. That's about all I can tell you," she said, managing to sound both efficient and sympathetic at the same time.

Finally, she came back with the words we had been yearning to hear. "The doctor is just finishing up now. Why don't you gather your belongings and come down to the recovery room?"

The surgeon, looking haggard and stern, materialized. "As expected, we had to take the kidney out. The tumor was so big it had twisted its way through his organs." Removing his glasses, he took extra long to clean them on his shirt scrubs. I wondered if he had forgotten about us.

Once he looked up and saw that Jackie and I were about to attack him if he didn't deliver the rest of the news, he continued. "We'll have to biopsy the tumor to find out what stage it is, but the good news is we got all of it and it appears to have been contained," he said, joining in the relief Jackie and I felt.

Attendants wheeled Connor in. He was so small, flush, and fluffy. The nurses were already giving him medication to take him out of his anesthesia-induced slumber. He coughed and opened his eyes. As instructed, we started giving him ice chips, which he initially rejected, angry and in pain as he was. After he fully awoke, he was moved into the pediatric intensive care recovery room and given more pain medication. My wife slept in a chair by his bed while I went out into the waiting room to find a sofa to sleep on. I drifted off to sleep relieved the surgery was a success.

I resolved to be a better father, not the inconsistent alcoholic parent I had been. As my boys aged and their emotions and moods became more complex, I had withdrawn, lacking confidence to help them through difficult times.

Connor was in the hospital for another week or so. Jackie and I rotated—she spent a couple of nights with Connor, and I stayed up in Westchester with Liam. Then I drove in, and we switched. After intensive care, Connor was transferred to the cancer ward in the adjoining Morgan Stanley Children's Hospital. Once he was discharged, he would be coming back a couple of times a month for chemo.

We played Uno, and I sometimes took him to the playroom where we rigged up a nerf basketball hoop or played air hockey. There were all kinds of volunteers coming through: comedians, singers, crystal and reiki experts, social workers with an array of games to choose from, and by far, the most beloved, the comfort dog. The dogs were not supposed to get up on the sick children's beds, but the owner, after whispering, "I'm not supposed to be doing this," usually let them hop up and cuddle.

We took to calling the now absent tumor the papaya because it was roughly that size and honored a delicious smoothie of orange juice, frozen strawberries and bananas and a papaya that I had been making the boys every summer for years.

One Saturday afternoon a couple of months after the cancer removal, I went to give blood at a nearby fire station in Westchester. As I was sitting with the needle in my arm and squeezing a ball to keep the blood flowing, I recalled stepping on that broken vase in the Kobayashi Mansion and blood pouring out of my foot onto my new sand-colored carpet. That image of a shard of black glass standing in the shag of the carpet digging into my foot conjured up that fragment of consciousness that had awakened in Japan. My time there was more in my thoughts these days, but I had no idea why.

But I had to pivot away from my confusing thoughts the minute I got home. Jackie was in a panic. Connor was ashen and having trouble breathing. We took him back to Morgan Stanley Children's Hospital where he had a whole battery of tests. He was cleared and sent home but woke up the next day in an even worse state.

By late afternoon he was pallid again and having periods where he gasped for breath. We took him to the emergency room of Northern Westchester Hospital in Mount Kisco, the local hospital where he had been born. The emergency room attending doctor stabilized him but said he needed to go back to New York to discover the precise issue.

Showing anxiety, he put Jackie and Connor in an ambulance for the hour ride to the New York City hospital we now knew so well. When Jackie saw me upon my arrival at the hospital the next day, she started crying uncontrollably, which was rare for her.

"They have been talking all night and now the main day surgeons are in," she explained.

"What's wrong with him?" I caught myself yelling. I resolved to be calmer, but I shivered in the heavily cooled air.

"It's bad. They need to figure what's wrong with him—and fast," she whispered unable to look me in the eye.

"He's going to be all right, right?" I asked. Having just arrived, I was an outsider trying to find my way in.

There was a long period of silence, which allowed the voices of doctors and nurses nearby to filter in. "They don't know." She was drained of color and barely able to speak.

They rolled him back into surgery, this one being more nerve wracking because of the uncertainty of the diagnosis. There was no watching *Frasier* this time around.

For some unknown reason after the surgery, a diaphragmatic hernia formed and eventually ruptured, providing a perfect gateway for all the dirty stuff from down below to rush into his lungs. The surgeons fixed the hernia, cutting back into the huge scar he already had on his stomach and putting in several drains near his lungs. The infection was so bad they explained they had to induce coma until they could get it under control. Thus, began a three-week vigil with the ultimate outcome in doubt.

During this time, I tried my best not to drink and was able to limit it to when I was at home, which for me was being abstemious. One Sunday I went in to spell Jackie for a couple of days. Connor was still in coma, and I gave him verbal updates on how the Boston Celtics were doing, including their wins and losses and leading scorers. Connor loved sports statistics. But otherwise, there was not much to do except read and watch TV, especially on weekends when there were fewer doctors and nurses popping in to have conversations.

Connor's situation was impacting Jackie and me differently but by this point in our marriage, we were not talking to each other about our fears, aspirations, or anything else percolating inside us. My drinking had erected a liquid wall that froze and became impermeable. It was sad—so sad that I suddenly got up and decided to get a bottle of rum from one of the half-dozen liquor stores within spitting distance from the front door of the hospital.

After drinking enough to pass out and sleep fitfully, I woke up early in the morning, cursed myself and decided to have some more to drink. When Jackie arrived later that morning, I pretended I was still sleeping next to Connor, but the trick didn't work.

"Get out of here and go sober up," she demanded. I obliged on the first part but not the second. Guzzling another bottle in the park, I passed out on the grass, telling myself I'd be sober when I woke up.

Some time passed and I decided I needed to get back to Connor's room, but I could not make it past the security guard. He sat me down in a chair near the front desk. After about ten minutes I started rushing across the lobby toward the elevators. He stopped me again.

"I can't let you in in this condition," he said sympathetically, but firmly.

"But my son needs me. He has cancer and almost died," I said slurring.

"It's tough having a sick son," he said, commiserating. "You said your wife is up there with him? Let me get a hold of her."

Jackie came down and was not too surprised to see me still drunk. I believe she thought Connor's plight should have been enough incentive for me not to drink but by this point in my drinking life, there was no external force that could keep me sober if I wanted to drink. The security guard let Jackie escort me in through the lobby to a courtyard. We sat on stone benches, and I felt a wonderful light summer breeze blow between us.

I said I was sorry about a hundred times and finally realized it was doing more harm than good. Jackie arranged for our friend Ed to come pick me up and take me home. I was so distraught I called my sister Jennifer in California and asked her to come and help me. Having dealt with drunks before, she agreed. Jennifer arrived on a redeye. She made sure I did what I had to do to stay sober, encouraged me, and spent time with Jackie and Connor. Her support gave me a little hope, not much, but in my state, I took anything I could get.

THE MOTORCYCLIST

2014

I STAYED SOBER FOR A WEEK OR SO but picked it up again. Now it was the July 4 holiday. It made sense to get in several days of drinking because Connor was coming home the next day and when he did, I had decided I was going to stop once and for all. That night I decided to watch the two *Conan: The Barbarian* movies back-to-back. They were perfect for heavy drinking because there was not much of a plot, and it didn't matter if you remembered anything about them.

Liam was off in his room playing video games and he would probably be doing that for the rest of the day. Before I resumed drinking after my nap, I called Jackie to confirm I'd be there to pick them up, and that Connor was alert and ready to come home after his induced coma. I figured if I could manage a run in the morning, the drive to the city to pick up Jackie and Connor would be tolerable.

Well, my hangover was of the colossal variety, and running was not an option. On top of that, the absolute last thing

I wanted to do was drive into the city. As a matter of fact, the thought of driving into the city made me positively ill.

Sitting on the counter near the sink was a small brown bag containing the prescription pain medication for Connor when he returned home. I'd picked it up from the pharmacy a couple of days before but hadn't paid much attention to what the medication was. Now I was curious.

Ripping the bag open, I saw a bottle of blue pills, but it was the plastic bottle with pink liquid that interested me. Looking at the label, I was surprised to see it said, "morphine." I hadn't realized it came in a liquid. Picking it up, I tossed it back and forth between my two hands. I stopped, opened the cap and smelled it.

I had never tried morphine but since this was for an eight-year-old boy, it could not have been that strong. I twisted open the top and took a nip. Nothing happened, so I then got dressed and readied myself to go pick them up. Just as I was headed toward the door, the morphine called out to me to remember it. I now felt a little better but not a lot, so I took two more big swigs.

As I was traveling up the driveway in Jackie's car, I was already hitting rocks on either side and jerking the steering wheel back and forth to steady the car, which seemed to have a mind of its own and did not want to be controlled. Once out of the driveway, I grazed trees on the driver's side of the road. As the second and third swigs of morphine kicked in, all sense of reality vanished and I sat in the car as if in a movie theater, watching a disaster I was powerless to stop unfold in front of me.

After turning off the street I lived on, I barreled down an angled, curling slope and then my car was stopped. At the base was one of those scenes that made living in Pound Ridge almost worthwhile: A gurgling brook flowing underneath the road and impeccably manicured properties covered in moss and ferns rolling up to each side of the street. But that was not what I was thinking: I stood in the middle of the road, hands in pocket, watching a motorcyclist struggle to rise from where his fallen bike lay.

I looked over his shoulder and I think I saw a young girl with curly brown hair spilling out from underneath her helmet staring at me. There was no judgment in her eyes but sadness.

I explained to the motorcyclist that I was terribly sorry but needed to get to the city to pick up my extremely sick son. I gave him one of my insurance cards and got back in the car. The imperative of getting to the hospital trumped all else.

I looked back one more time at the young girl and her neutral eyes were still trained on me. She had not moved but her despondency had deepened. I drove up the other side of the hill and around some snaky curves and the next thing I knew I was passed out. The car had landed on a stone wall, activating the air bag. There were what seemed like dozens of people around the car—one being a prominent journalist I knew from my work—and I was taken out by the EMTs.

Jackie's relatively new SUV was destroyed. I must have passed out again in the ambulance because when I awoke, I was handcuffed to a hospital bed and bandaged from where some-body had extracted blood. For the first time, I had sense enough to look down at my body. There was one small scrape on my leg. Despite the only minor injury, the doctor gave me instructions to get some rest and to be careful tomorrow as I might be sore.

Passing out again, I started coming to in a police car on the way to the Pound Ridge police station. Once I arrived, I was again handcuffed to some wooden bar, which seemed a bit medieval to me.

The Pound Ridge police force is housed in a small white building next to the town offices in a shady, mossy plot of land that backed up to a swamp. The force drove around in forest green and white SUVs, busying themselves with speeders, rabid raccoons and old people reporting suspicious vehicles on their quiet streets; at least that was my impression from the police blotter in the local newspaper.

One of my sons termed our town "the most boring place on the face of the earth," though the nickname among his friends for the locale was "The Dirty Ridge," as in a place full of filthy rich people. My suspicion was the police deliberately did not report the really bad stuff publicly. The Dirty Ridge seemed tranquil and bucolic on the exterior, but I surmised under the surface, it had the same problems as everywhere else.

Both Chief Ryan, a bear of a man who radiated calmness, and the officer who arrested me and drove me to the station, were present and immediately started peppering me with a lot of questions I was not quite able to answer yet. I do not remember being asked about the motorcyclist, which emboldened me to tuck it into the back of my brain and start pretending that maybe I imagined it.

They stopped questioning me after a while because I was still a blithering idiot. I had to arrange a couple of weeks later to be booked at another police station because I was too blitzed to give fingerprints and stand for a mug shot.

The chief turned to the other officer present. "I think he's okay to be uncuffed, don't you?" His tone of voice was not unfriendly. Perhaps the really bad stuff was over for the day? Once the cuff had been taken off my right wrist, I rubbed it with my left hand. I had been so nervous that I continually yanked it when I was answering questions, and it was red and sore.

"Let's get him some water, too," he said, turning to the other officer. The room was claustrophobically small, white and bright. I now agreed that the police needed a new facility. "Do you think you have a drinking problem?" the chief asked, looking straight at me.

"Yes. I've been trying off and on to get sober for over a decade, but I've always relapsed." Maybe getting sober was my ticket out of this mess, I thought, my first shred of hope that day.

"Have you tried AA?" Now that the official part of the interview was over, he turned compassionate.

My throat was incredibly dry and though I had not been noticeably injured in the car crash, my body now ached. "Yes, but I haven't stuck with it," I admitted. I had decided to be completely honest.

"Well, I know these guys in Bedford who have a really strong AA group," he said. "You ought to try it."

"Okay. I'll go," I affirmed, quite unaware of what I was committing to. The chief was being kind, when I probably didn't deserve it. But I would do whatever he suggested.

"I'll mention you to a couple of guys I know in that group," he said. He asked the other officer to drive me home. Silent all the way back, I was let off at the top of the driveway.

"I wouldn't drive anywhere tonight if I were you. You're still wobbly," he advised.

It was late afternoon by this time. I had left the house seven or eight hours ago. I pulled my phone out of my pocket for the first time since I'd left and saw all the messages from Jackie: I realized with horror that not only had I never showed up at the hospital to pick her and Connor up, but I had also not bothered to call her to tell her I wasn't coming. Already an advanced black belt in self-loathing, I don't think I ever hated myself more than I did in that moment.

As far as I can remember, I walked in and apologized. She knew an altered state was involved but I do not think she cared to know more. I lay in bed alone most of the day Sunday and tried to figure out how I had gotten into this mess and how I was going to get out. By Monday morning, I did not have any answers. While I had become intimately familiar with the feeling of waking up in terror, there were various degrees I had become acquainted with over the years. I had a high tolerance for pain, but that Monday morning was as close to unbearable as it had ever been.

Questions flashed into my consciousness and were immediately replaced by others.

How am I going to deal with my legal problems?

I had not talked to my insurance company yet. Was that a problem?

If I did hit a motorcyclist, was he hurt? Would I be charged with a hit and run because I did not stay? Could I be sued?

How am I going to fix everything with Jackie?

I destroyed Jackie's car. How was I going to afford to replace it?

Would news of my accident be public? Did I need to tell Goldman Sachs about it?

All that hit me in the face at one a.m. in the morning after I woke up from virtually no sleep. The worst part was I could not drink to make it all go away. I had to get sober once and for all this time.

In the end, I was charged with driving while ability impaired and one other vehicular charge; paid a large sum of money in fines and insurance surcharges; had my license suspended for a while; and attended a depressing drunk driving prevention class in Peekskill.

For some reason, I was not charged with anything to do with the motorcyclist, which made me even more comfortable pretending that it had not happened. Some of this is conjecture but the same officer who detained me that day informed me years later I had told him my son had died. That's not the type of expedient lie I would tell, but I could envision myself saying my son almost died, and in my still intoxicated state, messing up the delivery.

There was a horrible little story in our local paper two or three weeks later. It said I had caused two accidents and had been charged with drunk driving. I was saved from deeper embarrassment by the fact that the paper only existed in hard copy, preventing something from circulating broadly online.

I bought Jackie a new car and our relationship was passable on the surface, probably because I started going to AA and for the first time ever, was doing all the things I was supposed to be doing. Or at least I thought I was.

The incident with the motorcyclist continued to haunt me. When my insurance company, GEICO, asked for an explanation of what happened that day, I really couldn't give anything coherent. I test drove a few theories I had about what happened but when I started articulating them, they didn't seem to make much sense. The people I talked to were very efficient, but I could not divine whether they were sympathetic toward me or not.

One Saturday several weeks after the incident, a gentleman called saying he was the lawyer who represented the motorcyclist. I seem to remember the rider was visiting the area when his pleasant young life intersected with that of a sick and damaged person, me. He would have no way of knowing it, but if he wanted me punished, I obliged him in a way only I could do—an approach which inflicted the maximum amount of psychological suffering.

I did not speak with that lawyer but put him in touch with GEICO. Soon after, GEICO told me that though his injuries were not substantial, I should expect to be sued by the individual because he was requesting a large sum of money which GEICO was not willing to pay and that a lawsuit could happen anytime in the next three years.

I now appointed my mailbox my official torturer. Jackie usually picked up the mail at the top of our driveway, but she did so with a lag and not every day.

My routine became to either stop at the mailbox on my drive home from work at the end of my commute or walk up on Saturday or Sunday to check the mail. On each of those one thousand or more days, as I pulled down the rusted door of the mailbox, I imagined that the metal box held a communication seeking millions of dollars that would plunge me into financial ruin and the loss of marriage, job and shelter.

Terrified, I nevertheless asked GEICO for an update only every six months or so. Sometimes the other side had budged a little, but GEICO predicted a lawsuit right near the end of the three-year period. My anxiety, already at stratospheric levels, climbed still further. About a week before the three-year period ended, GEICO informed me the motorcyclist had settled.

I was relieved for about two hours, and then I caught myself searching for some familiar fear to latch onto. Fear had been my close companion for my whole life.

I could not give it up so easily.

BOTTOM NUMBER TWO

2017

THROWING MYSELF INTO AA AS NEVER BEFORE, I became part of the group the chief had mentioned and managed to stay sober for almost two years. The recipe was meetings every day and working with a sponsor on the Twelve Steps, which were ideally supposed to transform the way I approached life. My existence became more tolerable and my relationship with Jackie lost some of its toxicity.

But the bottom line was I still wasn't done drinking. I had had so many consequences and some part of me knew if I continued, I would lose my marriage as well. But I was compelled because I could not face myself sober. First, there was all the fear and terror I lived with every day. Second, there was the omnipresent gnawing in the bottom of my soul about who I really was, if anyone. And, who knew what lurked beneath those layers. I was afraid that it might even have been worse than what I was living with now.

Deceiving myself as every alcoholic or addict does, I figured I just had to exercise will power and everything would be fine. It wasn't, and two years later, Connor's cancer and the accident seemed like a distant memory. I had enough experience to know how to drink so I wouldn't get into any trouble, I began to tell myself.

In June of 2017, I came home extra drunk one night and when I called Jackie the next day from work as I gingerly did after I knew I had messed up, she told me not to come home. By this time, I was already staying in cheap New York hotels once or twice a week to mitigate the bruising commute, I told myself. In reality, if I stayed in the city, I could drink the way I wanted and not have to worry about pretending to be sober.

The problem with this seemingly perfect scenario was I was ridiculously cheap and did not like paying much for hotels. The cheapest in the city were in Chinatown along the Bowery, where the drunks and addicts did and do hang out. Using Expedia at the end of the day, I was able to get places for 60 bucks a night but hotels in New York should not go for 60 dollars. I got what I paid for: Bedbugs and horny tourists on a budget squeaking up the beds through the paper-thin walls all night.

How had a sunk to this? Is this who I really was? If so, was it worth continuing?

If I wanted to salvage my marriage, job, and sanity, I had to try something new. My longtime therapist who was by now mostly treating me for my alcoholism helped me reserve a room at a sober house called The Bridge on the Upper East Side of Manhattan. I checked in with Jimmy, one of the two people who ran the business.

"Gimme your bag," Jimmy demanded, with none of the respect I thought I should be getting for the thousands of dollars a month I was going to pay to stay.

"Why?" I was indignant. Two bedroom doors on the floor were partially open and I tried to peer in to see what my fate was going to be.

"I'm going to search it to see if you have any drugs." He was sitting at a table at the top of the stairs for the second floor. There was a safe behind him which contained who knew what.

"I take Naltrexone," I volunteered in a meek voice. This was a drug that prevented me from feeling buzzed if I drank booze. If it worked as advertised, there was no point in drinking.

"If that's all you're taking, you've nothing to worry about," he said, bending down to a box on the floor and fishing out a small plastic cup with a blue top and handing it to me.

"Go get me some urine," he commanded. "Oh, and leave the bathroom door open when you're filling the cup."

After turning over my specimen, I went out to an AA meeting. When I arrived back at the sober house, one of the other men, or inmates as I began to think of us, was preparing a meat stew.

Good, now I have an excuse for not joining them. I not only didn't want to be there, but I'd didn't want to bond with anybody in the house. It would just reinforce how low I had sunk. My room, which I shared with another person, was on the third floor. I lay down and looked out the window next to my bed. *How had I gotten here?* Like most things in life, very gradually and imperceptibly, with each decision to drink each day snuffing out a little part of who I was. I tried to sleep but Jimmy and the other men in the house, who were more boys than men, were watching a Yankees game. *How had I gotten here?*

* * *

I left early to go to work each day and after I was done, headed back uptown, and attended meetings on the Upper East Side with others from the sober house. It was humbling to say the least. At weekends, I went to stay in Westchester with Jackie and the boys. The sober house was a new level of commitment to sobriety and Jackie seemed hopeful, though I'm sure she was realistic, given how many times I had relapsed in the past.

Summer passed into fall. I moved out of the sober house after two months, feeling strong in my sobriety, and rented a sunny studio a block away. I wanted to move back to Pound Ridge but didn't discuss it with Jackie. I knew it was too soon.

As a birthday gift, Jackie had given Liam, who was now sixteen, two tickets for an Eric Clapton concert in September at Madison Square Garden. Liam was a teenager and as such generally preferred not to do anything in public with me, but we had previously had a bonding experience seeing The Who at MSG six months earlier. The big difference was I was sober for that but had decided to drink for the Clapton concert. Each time I drank now I rationalized it as just a one off, but I really was intent on destroying myself.

We arranged to meet at Grand Central Station shortly before the concert and I did what I normally did when I got out of work—I guzzled vodka. Unsteady on my feet, I remember thinking on the way to joining him that I had taken it a little bit too far.

The first words out of his mouth were, "Dad, are you okay?"

"I'm fine," I replied, my standard answer whenever I had had too much to drink.

"You're not walking very well," he observed, but was hesitant to openly challenge me.

"I hurt myself running this morning." By this point in my drinking career, lies upon lies flew out of my mouth like zephyrs.

We arrived at the concert venue incredibly early: The warmup band had not even started. I sucked down overpriced waters and began to sober up and thought I might just be able to handle being with Liam and not making a fool of myself. By the time Clapton started, I switched to vodka tonics.

I vaguely remember making a lot of stupid comments and

then the concert was over, and we made our way back to my apartment. Liam and I hung out in Pound Ridge Saturday waiting for Jackie and Connor to return home from a tennis tournament on Sunday. The liquor beast had been released and I drank, sleeping on and off during the day.

Cleaning up and food shopping before Jackie returned home, I picked up a pint of vodka for an emergency. Just as I had sat in my RAV4 in the Stamford parking garage a decade ago, I found myself at the top of the driveway in the same vehicle and went through my options. There were only two: Deal with my physical and emotional pain and wait to drink or get relief now and risk Jackie's ire. I chose the latter and drank down the bottle I had bought "just in case."

Bursting through the front door, Jackie took one look at me and shouted, "You're drunk. Get out of this house now. How dare you?"

"What? No, I'm not." I had to put up a weak defense. My butt was sunk deep into a recliner, and I was determined not to leave it until I had to.

"You know the consequences," she said. "Go back to the city."

I had to at least try to find a way to stay. "But I probably shouldn't drive."

"That's your problem. I don't know, get one of your AA friends to come pick you up," she suggested.

"I can't think of anybody. Okay, I am leaving," I said, finally getting out of the chair with some physical difficulty.

Though I knew I was completely in the wrong, there was a part of me that wanted to make her feel guilty. "I'll walk to the station and figure something out." I had no intention of doing that. I knew from experience my best bet was just to get out of the house. Besides, the rest of my vodka stash was waiting for me at the top of the driveway.

I gathered up my wallet, phone and a few other belongings and departed without saying goodbye to any of them. They were all ungrateful anyway. I pulled my vodka bottle out from the place in the stone wall I always left it and started staggering down the road. I took several deep pulls and decided I needed a nap. Jackie had told me to leave but she certainly only meant our property. There was a vacant forested lot that abutted ours and there, on a lush moss bed, I sat down and propped myself up against a tree. After resting and some more vodka, I'd figure things out.

I heard Jackie's car crunching the driveway's stone base and spinning out in a rush onto the road. She was gone for ten minutes and came back down the driveway. I gloated. *Perfect, she's feeling guilty for chucking me out of the house and went out looking for me.* This forested patch suited me, and I resolved to stay here as long as I could.

I dozed for a while and then I heard Liam and Jackie talking as they walked up the driveway. It took me a moment to realize that they were getting closer, and then I understood they were tracking my iPhone. They found me and I suddenly leapt up to defend myself.

"You told me to leave, and I did."

"You're still drinking. Give me that." She grabbed the bottle away and dumped it onto the dead leaves, which certainly had no use for it.

"Get back in our bedroom and don't come out until you leave next morning," Jackie instructed. It was not a desirable outcome for me to be back in the house. I cursed myself for not considering the iPhone tracker.

As we departed the woods and began heading down the driveway, Jackie walked ahead in disgust. She had been worried about me and was probably disappointed in herself for that. Silent, Liam walked beside me.

Finally, he spoke. "Mom is really, really mad at you."

"I know. I messed up." Uncharacteristically, my throat constricted, and I choked up a little.

Now, freed from my solitude and among people, I suddenly wanted to talk. "I want to kill myself." That comment would come back to haunt me, though at the time it seemed like a totally logical thing to say.

Jackie followed me upstairs and reminded me, "Do not come down in front of the boys in this state." And, she added something I did not quite understand at the time. "Make sure you send me the address of your apartment."

WHAT'S WARRANTED?

2017

WAKING UP THE NEXT MORNING, I did my usual commute to the city along with my special companions, self-revulsion, fear, and terror. Jackie and I did not talk Monday, but she emailed me again asking for my apartment address. I wracked my brains as to why she might need it but eventually gave up and sent it to her.

Later in the day I got a call from my old friend Chief Ryan of the Pound Ridge police department asking me to come into the station. I explained how busy I was and asked if it could wait until next week, to which he gently but firmly informed me it could not. Once inside the cramped station, I sat down. The chief quickly got to the point. Jackie was serving me with a protective order that generally did not permit me to go to what I still thought of as my home.

I was too shocked to respond. It was if he had ripped out one of my organs and I was staring at him with my last vestige of consciousness before I died.

"You understand you are not allowed on that property. Your children need to be there, and you need permission from Jackie," the Chief said, summarizing the order. No sympathy and kindness this time. It was all business. "This is really serious. You need to get some help."

"I will," I said, the sentence lacking energy and conviction. I was finally defeated.

"I'm telling you you're on the verge of not being able to see your kids unless court supervised," he continued. He wasn't sure I understood so followed up. "Do you really want to go there?"

I shook my head.

"You cannot go to that house without Jackie's permission. Are we clear?" I nodded. I had spoken a half dozen words through this entire exchange and wasn't about to change that as I stood to leave. The chief handed me a copy of the protective order and I walked out in the early fall air.

What did I do? I headed right back to the house to pick up some beach clothes I needed for my last trip to Montauk of the year. Soon after I returned to my office in Lower Manhattan, I received my first call from Westchester child services and was questioned extensively about what a horrible drunk parent I was. And they brought up my threatening to commit suicide in front of one of my children. Thursday afternoon I had my second interview with child services, this one face-to-face in Lower Manhattan.

At work so far that week, I had gone through the motions and tried to do what was necessary, but I was anything but productive. I also went to a couple of AA meetings with friends, but I didn't dare tell anybody I had relapsed or what had transpired at home. I just needed escape from my family, work, New York City, protective orders, child services, and, most importantly, myself. Fortunately, I was scheduled to go to Montauk Thursday night. On the way back from the second child services interview, I decided that despite what the chief said, I was going to get completely drunk during the three-hour train ride out to the southern tip of Long Island.

I bought a quart of Bacardi Limon as soon as I left the office and promptly drank a third in two quick gulps. So gluttonous was I for the liquor to make its way quickly into my bloodstream I was out of breath when I pulled the bottle away from my lips. Stepping outside after the subway ride to Penn Station, I topped my buzz off and headed down the station stairs to the Long Island Railroad. I noticed a phone message I had missed on the subway and played it back.

"Mr. DuVally, this is the Pound Ridge police department. I need you to come to Pound Ridge tonight in regard to a violation of the order of protection you were issued, and Chief Ryan explained to you. Please give us a call back and let us know what time you will be able to come up here tonight. Charges will be filed against you; you will be placed under arrest, and you will be arraigned before a judge. I would bring 500 to 1000 dollars for bail. If you choose not to come up here tonight, we will have an arrest warrant drawn out for you and we will come down and pick you up at your job. Please give us a call. Thank you very much."

There had already been numerous times I thought my life was insolvent, but this took the stakes to a new level. I thought of going to Montauk anyway and saying I hadn't received the message in time, but I could only imagine the green and white Pound Ridge SUVs crisscrossing New York State searching for me.

I resolved to head up to Pound Ridge and face the inevitable destruction of my life. Walking the 20 minutes it took to get to Grand Central Station, I stopped at every coffee shop I passed and purchased bottles of water and coffees. I had to sober up quickly. After the train ride to Stamford, I hopped in my car and drove the half an hour to the police station.

When I knocked on the door of the police station it was nine and though I did not feel completely sober, I thought I could pull it off.

I was met by the officer who had arrested me for the DWI four years earlier and his contempt for me had not lessened. Ushered into the room with which I was now familiar, I noticed the chief wasn't around. He soon joined us though, which was probably the first good thing that happened to me that evening.

He took one good look at my eyes and his nose sniffled. "You're not drunk, are you?"

I hesitated and with the greatest concentration I could muster to pronounce every word properly and clearly, I said, "I had a little to drink. I was going to Long Island, and it's been a tough week."

"How much?" the other officer asked. He continued to make it abundantly clear during the conversation that he liked playing bad cop. And why not? I don't think he had ever seen me sober.

I stayed silent.

"Oh, Mr. DuVally, Mr. DuVally, did you go over to the house on Tuesday after I read you the protective order?" the chief asked in exasperation. Not in uniform, he obviously had already been home for the evening and had been trying to enjoy time with his family.

"Yeah. I just went to pick up clothes," I said and then getting animated at the thought I could escape the charge, I realized I had a text to Jackie telling her I was coming over. She had not objected, proof of exoneration, I explained.

He looked at my iPhone. "She didn't acknowledge it either," he said, completely extinguishing the flicker of hope I had had a moment earlier.

"You know you just committed a felony?" It was a rhetorical question, as they all were, and I did not want to answer any of them.

"It also looks like you showed up in my station drunk. Did you drive here?" My panic level rose along with my mounting troubles. I wondered how I hadn't yet exploded, rending my body into bits. "Is there more alcohol in your car?" the other officer asked, sneering at me.

"No."

"Do we have permission to search your vehicle?" the chief asked.

"Yes, there's nothing there." One of the few wise things I had done before driving up was to pitch the rest of the Bacardi Limon bottle.

After a time, the two of them came back. Chained again to my now familiar medieval bar, I was not going anywhere.

In the end, after a lot of conversation, including one with a judge, the chief booked me and charged me with violating the protective order, a felony. I was not charged with DWI even though I was over the limit and had driven my car drunk. Again, the chief took pity on me and put me in touch with a local defense attorney.

While I appreciated the break he had given me, I had no doubt that was partly for Jackie's sake. If I got tossed out of my job at Goldman Sachs the family would suffer along with me. Whatever his motivation, I simultaneously felt grateful and undeserving.

I paid my bail. On the way up, I had pictured myself sprawled on the floor of the jail with no hope of freedom. This was a better outcome than I had a right to expect. It was 11 now and one of the officers drove me from the police station to Mount Kisco, where I somberly boarded a train back to the city.

I was convinced in the police station that I would never take a drink again, but my nerves were so raw I stopped at a dive bar near my apartment in the city.

* * *

I went back to Pound Ridge on Saturday. It was six days after I had been thrown out of the house and what a six days it had been. I arrived early. The boys were still sleeping but Jackie, uncharacteristically, was already downstairs pacing. She got right to the point.

"I want a divorce," she said with a conviction and finality that shocked me.

Reflexively, I begged. "Come on, you can't mean it. Please don't."

"How many times can we go through this? I am completely serious this time." There was no sympathy. She was shaking with anger.

"I know I can stop drinking for good now," I responded, hoping for one last miracle. Outside the sliding glass doors, the leaves had just begun to change. The maples in the backyard were showing signs of their fall crimson blush.

"I really hope you do, and the boys do, too. We're rooting for you," she said, ratcheting down her ire. I involuntarily scoffed.

"We're your biggest fans, but it's going to be from a distance because you're not welcome here anymore." Silence. The dog snuggled up to me, but I pushed him away. I was being cast away and did not want any physical warmth from another living creature.

I paused. A part of me wanted to keep arguing but a part of me knew that this was it. If the marriage had meant more to me, I would have stopped drinking earlier. I bit my tongue. It was hard but it was an early sign that despite relapsing, some of what I had learned in AA stuck. For the first time in a long time, I looked at the situation from Jackie's perspective. It was much more humane to let her be free of me.

"I have to tell you I feel like an idiot having stayed with you that long," Jackie said. The knife was stuck in, and I just had to let it penetrate and rip at the shreds of my heart. "The worst part of it was when Connor was sick and when my mother was ill, I could not completely focus on them. I had to worry about whether you were drunk and able to take care of the kids. You robbed me of a chance to experience my feelings."

Amid the stillness of the room, I blinked.

* * *

That fall was a constant trek up to Westchester for appearances in family court in White Plains related to the protective order and to Pound Ridge court to deal with the criminal violation of the order. The pair of lawyers I needed to handle these two separate issues did not come cheaply.

They kept telling me I could still come out of this okay, but all bets were off the table if I showed up back at the house drunk. Part of a more detailed protective order required me to use a device called Soberlink, a breathalyzer that was programed to send test results to Jackie every time I was to have contact with my sons. I ended up utilizing the device for almost two years, yet another dose of humility.

There was a mix-up in the drafting of language of the more detailed protective offer and I was now prevented from not only going up to Pound Ridge but even talking on the phone to Jackie, which made everyday tasks difficult because our lives were still very intertwined.

By staying sober and humble over the next couple of months, I partly regained my family's trust and was allowed to take Connor to his age group's national tennis tournament in Tucson over the Christmas holidays at the end of 2017. Connor had a great time competing and hitting with his friends. I tried to be a more attentive father, was grateful to be sober and even got in some spectacular runs amid the cacti in several national parks.

It seemed like I was on my way.

SNAIL TRAILS

2018

I HAD BEEN WARNED MANY, MANY TIMES that isolation was the enemy of recovery. Jackie's decision to divorce me, and my legal troubles were receding to a place in my head and did not plague me every waking hour. It was January and I had three-plus months of sobriety under my belt. I was starting to believe that I just might make it this time.

On the Friday before President's Day weekend, I was out at a meeting that was usually followed by fellowship: dinner together with other alcoholics and addicts. Fellowship forced us to talk to other people and taught us how to have fun without booze and drugs. I was supposed to go out to eat with a large group to have Chinese.

I shouldn't have been squirmy that night, given I had been to a meeting every night that week and I had gone for fellowship after every meeting, but I was.

On nights like these, I typically wouldn't get back to my cramped fourth floor walk-up studio apartment on the Upper

East Side of Manhattan until 9:30 or 10 p.m. I also liked to go running in the morning, which required me to get up at 4:45 a.m. or so before work. This schedule was not a good recipe for a healthy amount of sleep, but it was keeping me sober, which was really what counted.

I had a service commitment that Friday night, which meant I was required to read the mid-meeting announcements. Most AA gatherings take place in church basements, just as they are depicted on TV. This one was in the daycare section of the church basement and harshly lit by long glowing bulbs.

Chairs were arranged in a large circle with additional rows where the room permitted, and those rows were needed given this meeting could draw upward of 75 people. What was particularly nice about this group was it attracted a wide age and sober time spectrum.

I did what I was supposed to do, but as the meeting was ending at 7:30 p.m., my brain grew itchy. No matter how hard I tried through positive thinking, I could not scratch the irritation away. *I'm tired. I have done enough fellowship this week and I am going home.*

Fuck fellowship.

I walked out of the meeting without saying farewell to any of my friends. Heading up York Avenue where the church was, I avoided Second Avenue, which was the street I usually took. *The sidewalks are less crowded. This makes more sense.* Passing a liquor store, I stopped and peered in the window but could not locate any pint bottles of the citrus-infused rum I liked. I decided to go in just to make sure they had some behind the front counter, not that I intended to buy any.

But, once inside the warm, cozy, wood-paneled shop, I saw that pint bottles of Bacardi Limon were just on lower shelves I couldn't see. Once I eyed them, they began winking at me in the light and, without hesitating, I asked for one. I was peeling off the cheap tin top before I left the store, and with that first slug, nearly four months of sobriety vaporized.

An economist would call my state *pent-up demand* for alcohol, and so after a taste, I wanted a gushing, endless stream of booze. Pausing every couple of streets, I must have stopped a half dozen times between the church and home, drinking what seemed like heated knives but the blades were so pleasant, piercing my brain and allowing all those worries, fears, and resentments to dribble out onto the street around me.

The bottle was gone by the time I neared home, but liquor stores abounded on the Upper East Side, just as they did all over New York. By now, I decided I was going to drink for the next couple of days, so I needed a half-gallon. Unable to decide between rum and vodka, I bought one of each.

I missed many things about giving up booze; hangovers were not one of them. After four months, I became used to feeling rested when I awoke—no throbbing head, acidy stomach, and general hatred of the world. But when I roused myself the next morning, my blankets were twisted in knots at the bottom of my bed and my sheets clammy wet, leaving me wondering if I had urinated in my sleep.

Now that I had tossed away my sober time, I decided I was going to start drinking early. Vodka and orange juice at 8 a.m. did the trick but I needed to slow down if I wanted to do anything constructive during the day. On errands and a low-quality short run, I decided I could not blow off the whole weekend. I was taking Myla to the New York Philharmonic on Saturday night. I had also bought tickets to a college basketball game in Providence and, for some reason, had invited my mother.

It was all cool and doable.

Of course, I also needed to go to AA meetings just as I typically did on the weekend. That gave me pause. Perhaps

I'd take a little vacation from AA but go back after I returned from Providence.

If I drank until three or four p.m., took a two-hour nap, had a nip before I went out, I would be in fairly good shape, I reasoned. Once upon a time, I had been exceptionally good at this type of planning but as my drinking career stretched into its fourth decade, Demon Rum's impact on me was increasingly unpredictable.

I made it to the concert, dozed off during the classical performance (all the old people did anyway) and was able to sneak in a quick double rum and Coke at intermission, which tided me over until the concert was finished. I bade my daughter farewell. I was virtually sober now (or so I told myself) and ready to drink from the two half-gallon bottles I had bought the day before. Closing the door to my apartment was the last thing I remember of that evening.

I woke up early. In less than 36 hours of drinking, I was already back to my old drunk routine of sleeping for no more than three or four hours. The hangover tolerable, I declared myself able to make it up to Stamford by train to pick up my car and navigate the three-hour drive to Rehoboth.

Packed and ready to go, I hesitated. The game wasn't until President's Day Monday afternoon, so I could drink today, head up early tomorrow and then drive home Tuesday as I initially planned. Sure, it would be a short trip, but a good one because I was going to relax on Sunday. With that decision made, at 7 a.m., I took my first drink of the day to take the edge off my hangover. As the vapor rose into my head, I mused how enjoyable and productive today would be. Thus, began my next, and hopefully last, trip down the rabbit hole.

There are only snippets of memory of the next four days: Purchases of two pizzas and several more half gallons of rum and vodka; panicked inability to find the rum I had brought into the house; and incessant texts and calls from family and AA friends. I listened and read them on the first day but by the second day, I completely gave up.

Once when I went on a rum run, I could not open the front door to my apartment building and fell on my face, opening gashes in my forehead and cracking my two front teeth. Drinking was not so glamorous anymore.

And, then there was the cutting knife. It was a very sharp model I bought at Whole Foods that I used to chop all my vegetables. I had been fantasizing about killing myself off and on for 30 years. At first, I gently ran it up and down my wrists, not breaking the skin but leaving white trails.

Almost every other time I had been really bombed, I could generally assume I would wake up and have to deal with a debilitating hangover and the other consequences of the night before. But this time might be different. I had to really cut my wrists for the first time, and at the very least, draw some blood, to show everybody that this was serious—an escalation.

This time, I didn't know how this bender would end.

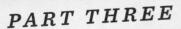
PART THREE

HOPE

"A well-thought-out story
doesn't need to resemble real life.
Life itself tries with all its might to
resemble a well-crafted story."

—Isaac Babel, *My First Fee*

LAZARUS OF BETHANY

2018

THAT FRIDAY IN JANUARY, I was transported to the darkest and terror-filled place I had ever been—beyond the horrors of my childhood, the binge drinking in Japan, the felonies and arrests, and my own wife and sons' loathing of my disease— but it was a location I needed to visit.

After ignoring the phone for five days, I finally picked it up and asked for help. Support came and I was given a choice of detox or a psych ward, and I chose the former. A friend spent the day getting me a bed and making sure they accepted my insurance. Like a slug in the fresh morning dew, I had left trails of blood, feces, and urine all over my apartment those last few days. My friend helped me clean up, bandaged my wrists, and then drove me to detox.

In recovery, we're told to treasure these low points in our life because it is at these junctures when we are utterly spiritually and morally bankrupt, that the tender shoots of recovery poke through the thawing ground. I had my last drink on January 18, 2018. The alternative is incomprehensible.

I found myself in the middle of nowhere New Jersey, a town named Union. The detox was called Serenity, but I was empty of that now. A nice, young lady festooned in body piercings and tattoos asked, "Are you okay?"

"No, I need medication and sleep," I muttered and lay back down on the cheap plastic sofa in reception.

"We're working on getting your bed ready," she said, and to demonstrate her concern, she picked up the phone and asked somebody when I could move into my room.

Time passed. She looked over at me with genuine sympathy as I lay curled in an angry ball, detesting every cell in my body.

"It'll get better," she said passionately and reassuringly.

Despite my lack of response, she added, "I know you can do this. I have faith in you."

I didn't have faith in myself, but her words opened a small crack in my façade of grief. That's not something I recognized at the time, though, and I spent a miserable six days there at a cost of $16,000 to my insurance company. The stay there was both interminable and fleeting.

Transported to a room with another surly recovering alcoholic or addict, I was soon told I would be moving again. Perhaps Mr. Sullen complained but I did not care because they moved me into my own accommodation. There was a special cleaning smell there that I will never forget, particularly in the bathroom. It was like somebody mixed generic versions of Lysol and Clorox and then sprayed Pledge on top of it.

After a couple of days, as the haze from my stupor began to dissipate, I remembered I had never called in sick to Goldman Sachs, despite having been AWOL for the week. Finally getting through to the right person in human resources, I explained that I was very ill and needed to take a leave of absence. Fortunately, all true. Not permitted to use my phone for more than five minutes, I called Jackie and a few other people and told them I was safe. It sounded strange using that word, but it was the right word. I was safe, at least while I was in here.

There were certain times of day I had to go to the pharmacy to get my meds and there were a lot of them—a half cup's worth. It was a detox, after all. I knew I could not drink anymore but the pills were welcome and adequate to trigger the kind of stupor where I did not have to think about anything.

I had been convinced to return to the sober house for a third time upon discharge and Jimmy arranged for a car to take me back from Serenity. Except for that one brief time, I had not had access to my iPhone while at the detox. I spent the trip back to Manhattan looking at all the messages from people who assumed I might be dead. As the New York skyline grew in front of me I was flooded with dread—I had let down everybody in my life and I was likely to lose my job to boot. I tried to respond to any messages from friends who might not have heard I was not dead. "I was sick and in a bad place but I'm safe now."

I was a bundle of jangled nerves but as soon as I got to the sober house, Jimmy said, "We're going to see your therapist."

"I'm tired. Can't we do that tomorrow?" I whined. I just wanted to curl up in bed, take some of the drugs I had been sent home with and fall asleep.

Weak with rubbery legs from the lithium, I knew the subway would make me sick, but Jimmy insisted.

My therapist, Michael, had been a drug and alcohol addiction counselor for one of the outpatient rehabs I'd been to. He had now set up a private practice on the Upper East Side.

"We're going to do things differently this time," he said emphatically raising his arms and eyebrows at the same time. "You need to surrender completely."

I was defeated, utterly and completely anyway.

"What do you want to do for outpatient?" Michael asked,

pausing. I followed his glance over at Jimmy who was bouncing his feet up and down and looking like he was going to bound out of his chair any minute.

"I want to go to Hazelton," I declared, adding "Something different that I haven't tried before." *Where did that come from? That was the most emphatic sentence I uttered in the last week.*

"We're on a roll. What about drugs?" he asked.

I didn't know where he was going with this, and I suddenly felt very weary. Comparing myself to a shark, I always told myself I'd die if I stopped moving. But, for the first time in my life, I didn't want to even stir. I wanted to be unconscious all the time if that was possible.

My therapist explained that he believed I had been self-medicating with alcohol all these years to treat my depression. Throughout my life, I steadfastly denied being depressed because I didn't know what would have made me depressed.

After all, I never had trouble getting out of bed. Even if I was hung over, I always accomplished everything I was supposed to. If I admitted I was depressed, we'd have to explore what was making me depressed and I didn't want to know what was behind that trap door.

But perhaps I did.

"Don't you think it's time we actually tried something?" my therapist asked emphatically, shocking me out of my musings.

"I'm willing," I said, spitting out the magic phrase.

After an aborted attempt at Zoloft, which kept me up for four consecutive nights, my new psychiatrist settled on Wellbutrin and Seroquel to treat my depression and help me fall asleep. The problem with Seroquel though was that it took me hours each morning to shake off the lethargy it triggered. And that was on top of the general ennui that essentially kept me in bed for much of the morning. This was the first time in my life I felt debilitating depression.

Jimmy's partner at the sober house, Lance, was usually in the living room in the morning when I trudged down the stairs from my bedroom. Jimmy was liquid energy, but Lance was calm personified. He was tall and dressed in black most of the time. Cuddling his bulldog, who smelled a little like my sickness, was one of the few tasks that made me happy early on.

He wouldn't really talk much but just him there, drinking Diet Coke with CNN on, made my life a tad less heavy for the fifteen minutes I stayed in the room; it ended when I asked for an extra Klonopin to steady my nerves.

I had enrolled in intensive outpatient counseling at Hazelton in Chelsea. This was the fourth time in my life I had tried outpatient, but the first time I was going four days a week for three hours at a time. I managed to get out of bed and trek downtown for the sessions each day, but I sat glowering in my chair defiantly not participating in the group discussions and workshops.

I met periodically with my psychiatrist, who was on the Upper East Side but all the way over on East End Avenue, by Carl Schultz Park. After each session, I walked over to the railing high over the roiling East River and fantasized about jumping. *What would it be like to hit the frozen waters alive, go under and not come up again? If I survived the initial fall, would I have an overwhelming desire to live? But if I did, would I be dead by the time I made it to shore?*

I clutched the railings not entirely sure whether I would vault over.

At the start of February, there were two matters that required my immediate attention: Taxes and Iceland. Every time I picked up my mail or printed a relevant tax correspondence, I stuffed it into folders and when I went through the folders and thought of having to get everything organized to bring to my accountant, I panicked. So, one Sunday, I resolved to go down to my office in the hope that the professional setting would allow me to organize all the forms. Given that I was on leave, I felt I was breaking into the office as I went through the turnstiles. But I did not transform into a pillar of salt and actually made some progress.

Travel was a bigger problem. I had decided for February vacation to take Liam, then 16, and a friend to Iceland. Having been numerous times, I had booked an ambitious agenda that included hot springs, glacier climbs, ice cave excursions and snorkeling in glacial run off. Having already disappointed everybody close to me, the thought of having to tell my son we couldn't go, coupled with the effort to cancel all the reservations I'd made filled me with dread. I waited until two weeks before the trip, hoping against hope that I would recover in time. I did not, and on advice from all my friends, I pulled the plug. Liam was understanding, at least on the surface. My boys never talked about my drinking while it was going on.

My daughter, Myla, was a constant companion to me during these times. We met at Café Bleriot on the Upper East Side, and I sat there looking down at the floor, raising my head only to drink my coffee. At the time, I considered being with any person and trying to talk a crushing burden, but I realize now sitting with her and her unconditional love helped me heal.

Sometime in February, I decided I did not want to die anymore. I don't remember the exact day, but my insides just felt different. Also, I now knew that if I wanted to live, I could not drink anymore. Beyond that, I had no expectation my life would improve.

Once out of detox, I contacted Goldman Sachs again to nail down the particulars of medical leave and to my surprise the company was very accommodating. My befuddled alcoholic mind had dreaded the worst. Jackie had been contacted by Goldman Sachs' security during my AWOL week, fueling fears of termination. I found out later that in addition to Goldman Sachs, three different police departments—the New York City police, the Pound Ridge police, and the Rehoboth (Massachusetts) police—were all involved in trying to locate me during that week.

I returned to my job part time in the middle of March, working four days a week in the morning, going to rehab in the afternoons, and spending a full day at Goldman Sachs on Fridays.

On my first day back, I'd not been in my chair for ten minutes when Goldman's folksy communications head, Jake Siewert, stepped into my office and closed the door. "How are you doing? We're glad you're okay."

"I'm happy to be back," I lied.

"Why don't you lighten your responsibilities," he suggested. I didn't know what that meant or why he brought it up, but I didn't care. If I didn't get this early recovery right, I wasn't going to make it.

Meanwhile, at Hazelton's intensive outpatient, everyday started with something called process group, where each of us checked in and told the group what was going on in our lives. After that activity finished, we focused on somebody in the group who had something extraordinary going on in his or her life. The first three weeks there I said little beyond what was required of me. I kept my coat on because it was so cold and rested my head on the top of the back of the chair.

"Michael, you've been very quiet," the group facilitator kindly mentioned.

"My life sucks," I said with finality, hoping to head off any attempts to get me to elaborate. This is what I had done each time I had gone to outpatient. I knew such animosity was not constructive, but my mood told me this was how to behave.

One day, something changed. I began to care about other members in the group, particularly one woman who made my defiance look like acquiescence. Giving advice in a compassionate way was encouraged, and I began to do that for others in the group (not for myself, of course, because I still did not have any self-empathy yet).

Recovery seemed excruciatingly slow at times and at others was like bamboo growing in Kyoto—visible over the course of days. A scintilla of hope grazed my awareness from time to time as I entered March. It was not there most of the time and when hope did appear, I tended to discount it because how many times had I stopped drinking only to pick up again?

By now, I was able to get out of bed though the fogginess of the Seroquel persisted. My routine consisted of an AA meeting at 7:15 in the morning, followed by yoga, and then breakfast. Chores and errands were next and then a five-mile run to outpatient, followed by another meeting and yoga or fellowship afterwards. It took me a while to develop this schedule but once I had, I marveled at how full my days had become. Even I could not deny that I was getting better.

At first, I noticed that the depth of my self-hatred was shallower and not constant. And every once in a while, there were pulses of something akin to tolerance of self. I could foresee a day where I might actually like myself sometimes.

These feelings were so alien to me I couldn't process them, but I didn't have to. I just had to let them be and hopefully they would grow.

I hit my 90 days of sobriety in mid-April and spoke about my experience at a couple of meetings. Making myself vulnerable by sharing the intimate details of my past was initially paralyzing. After all, I had spent my whole life fearing people would reject me. My story had become much more interesting in the last four years as I built up a store of degrading and horrific experiences. It was powerful and sometimes helpful to others listening that I could throw in fantasy details about jumping in a river, drinking morphine intended for my cancer-stricken son, hitting a stone wall with my car, or slashing my wrists.

I began to settle back into Goldman Sachs, and reluctantly accepted the new reality that the upward mobility that characterized most of my career was over. I had been working the Twelve Steps of Alcoholic Anonymous for the second time with my sponsor, a spiritual man who generously gave of his time to not only teach the program but to nurse me back to health. We met in his office in Midtown and read through the first 164 pages of the *Big Book*, AA's bible.

Step Three was said to be the most important one—the one where we fully capitulated and admitted that we could not run our lives without the help of Higher Power. There was a part of Step Three called the Third Step promises, which discussed how life can be transformed if we stopped trying to run every aspect of our life and turned that over to a Higher Power. According to the AA *Big Book*:

> "When we sincerely took such a position, all sorts of remarkable things followed. We had a new Employer. Being all powerful, He provided what we needed, if we kept close to Him and performed his work well. Established on such footing we became less and less interested in ourselves, our little plans, and designs. More and more we became interested in seeing what we could contribute to life. As we felt new power flow in, as we enjoyed peace of mind, as we discovered we could face life successfully, as we became conscious of His presence, we began to lose our fear of today, tomorrow or the hereafter. We were reborn."

I had previously read this section a couple dozen times, but never instinctively understood what it meant. But, this time, sitting on a plane on the way back from a trip accompanying our CEO Lloyd Blankfein to the Goldman Sachs Dallas office, I had the visceral realization that for the first time, I wanted to have some other force in charge of my life. This was my spiritual awakening and it filled me with ecstasy, elation, and hope.

There was nothing mystical about the plane or the business trip I was on. The stirring of my spirit only occurred because I was willing for it to happen, whereas each time in the past when I worked Step Three my heart wasn't open. This experience propelled my recovery into hyperdrive.

Five months later at work I had a sudden desire to buy makeup.

THE WORLD JUST GOT BIGGER

2019

AFTER I GOT SOBER IN JANUARY of 2018 and started taking recovery seriously, my life got big, fast. It was as if Michael had died that day in my apartment so that Maeve could live and thrive. For the first time in decades, I had more friends than I knew what to do with and people *wanted* to spend time with me.

This was disorienting because at the very end of my drinking in my mid-50s, my world was very small, and I was all alone. My sole companions were bottles of vodka and rum stuffed in my work bag, into boots in my closet, under the seat of the car or in a stone wall at the top of my driveway. I had interacted with human beings every day, but I was just going through the motions. The reality of my life was I was just flitting from one distasteful task to another, and by mid-morning, yearning for that first drink of the evening.

My first summer as Maeve in 2019, just months after my coming out at Goldman Sachs, I spent a fair amount of time on the tip of Long Island in Montauk. Lolling on the beach in a tan bikini I bought at Athleta, I refrained from venturing into the ocean because I hadn't figured out how to "look" feminine coming out of the water, and at that point in my life, looking good was more important than swimming.

As a matter of fact, I went from indifference to my looks to quite vain very quickly. I jogged every day from Ditch Plains where I was staying to Montauk Point and back, a good nine miles, and then did yoga. Besides exercise, sunning and getting a good tan was important. It was all quite indulgent, but it helped me feel good about myself.

Sprawled out on my green and orange blanket at Ditch Plains beach, I watched the surfers bobbing in the breakwater. Jimmy, who co-ran The Bridge sober house I stayed at in Manhattan, came up from behind and plopped a beach chair next to me. His summer gig was trying to fill a sober share near "Ditch" as the locals called it.

"See, this is what you need—being around sober people and going to meetings together," Jimmy declared, draining his bottle of kombucha. Jimmy tried to cultivate the surfer look, with hair down to his shoulders and a tan so deep it didn't seem real. He said "dude" a lot, but everybody here except me seemed to say it as well.

I was thinking of getting lunch at the trailer parked in the lot by the beach called the Ditch Witch. The vegetarian wraps were excellent though the prices made New York City seem cheap. I laid back down, adjusting my bikini so it fit just right over all the parts it was supposed to. As usual, I was self-conscious when I went to take my outer coverings off and unveiled my bikini body for the first time. Looking around, I scanned the beach nearby to see if anybody was staring at me, but everybody was either lying in the sun or sitting up talking to friends.

I inspected my body, now hairless after several sessions of laser and sporting swelling breast buds courtesy of hormones for the last eight months, and decided it looked better as a girl's than it ever did as a boy's. My penis was still there but if I tucked it back, nobody seemed to notice. I had already decided it was coming off next year anyway.

"You'll go to the meeting in Montauk with us tonight, right, Michael?" Jimmy said in more of a statement than a question.

"It's Maeve," I corrected, smiling and sitting up. It would take a lot to upset me at this place. There were a couple of dozen surfers to my left, sitting comfortably offshore waiting for just the right wave. In front of me, children played in the water and a young couple hit a ball with paddles. It was such a calm, comforting scene I felt my heart pulse, and I sighed.

"What are the meetings like out here?" I asked just out of curiosity, not that it would have impacted my decision to go.

"Good sobriety, a lot of old timers," Jimmy said, swishing a toothpick around his mouth.

"This is one of the few beaches I've visited that I haven't ever been drunk on," I said, pausing and looking at the sun until my eyes hurt. "It's a nice feeling."

Jimmy didn't say anything. After pausing, he declared, "I'm going to talk to somebody I know over there." He had the tendency to suddenly move on. I didn't take it personally.

Alone now, I remembered the last time I had felt such peace on a beach. My mother used to take us to my grandfather's modest beach house near Scarborough Beach in Rhode Island when I was eight or nine. It was in a camp of seasonal summer homes about a quarter of a mile from the beach, which beckoned to come quickly and build sandcastles, body surf, and collect starfish, hermit crabs and periwinkles off the jetty rocks nearby.

Relatively close to Rhode Island's main population centers, it teemed with scents of Coppertone, cigarettes, and hot dogs. If we were fortunate enough to be brought back to the beach at dusk, we soaked in a far different scene. People threw balls for their dogs and old men moved their metal detectors back and forth over the sand in the hope of discovering treasures. One time, I looked out shortly before the sun set and a school of small fish all jumped in the air at the same time, churning the water a deep purple. For a long while after they moved out to sea, I couldn't take my eyes off the place where it happened. That was one of the last times I felt the exquisiteness of the beach, until this summer in Montauk.

On my runs up to Montauk Point, sometimes I detoured off Montauk Highway onto various paths that ran through stunted trees and vines thriving in the wet salty air. Right across from the Deep Hollow Ranch riding stables on the Montauk Highway was a path that advertised a beach at its end, though the trail was hemmed in by sharp-leaved scrub brush. I followed its twists and turns, dark and light, and its mud, which was navigated by conveniently laid wooden planks. I silently cursed myself for not slathering my legs with tick repellent as this was an epicenter of Lyme's Disease.

As far as I could see from the highway, the path was mostly flat to the ocean, but that masked a series of steep ascents and descents once I got into the drooping vine maze. As I neared the water, I realized I had dropped quite a way and therefore would have to ascend to get to the bluffs that overlooked the ocean. I kept climbing and it looked like any minute I would break out of the coastal bushes, thick with the smell of cloying berries. I had heard some surfers carried their boards through this path to the beach. That didn't seem possible to me.

When I reached the top of the bluff, I was alone. To the right, around a curve, I could see Ditch Plains beach and to the left, the magnificent and solemn Montauk Point Lighthouse. I followed a slightly beaten path through the dune grass to the beach and squatted on a barnacle-coated rock, my gift being a salt spray immersion without taking a direct hit from the waves.

Rocks littered the water and I doubted anybody could really surf here. I took my sneakers and socks off and waded out to my knees. I would have liked to get soaked but the 67-degree ocean temperature was doing the trick of cooling me down. My feet trod on smooth hockey puck-sized rocks that covered the sea floor here. They clacked against each other as the top ones tumbled over the next layer whenever the water receded after a wave. Returning to my barnacled stone, I let my ears feast on the soothing rock symphony.

This moment would be even closer to perfect if I wasn't alone, I thought. I wanted to be with another girl to share the beauty here.

She came up behind me stealthily; I could feel her cool breath on my neck before I could see her. I turned with a jolt, but she got no closer and walked past me into the surf until she was waist deep. She had a surprising agility despite the rocks. Then she turned toward me.

She was of average height, with a rich red hair, milk-white skin and beautiful freckles all over her body. I think her eyes were green but that could have been the reflection off the water. She had a rich, full body with ample curves. Her clothes were tattered, and the thick brown gelatinous seaweed supplemented her skimpy wardrobe. She was both disheveled and put together perfectly at the same time.

"I've been waiting for you," she said though her mouth didn't move. Her words were just inside my head, and eventually I found I could communicate with her that way, too.

"I wish I looked better—more feminine," I said. She was

the shape of near perfect womanhood, which I would never have, especially when I was running. I had brawny legs from hitting the roads daily and I covered my wig with a baseball cap when I ran. To cloak my masculinity more, I usually put on some makeup.

"You look beautiful," she said, her eyes shining. I stared into them, now convinced they must be green or maybe greenish blue. The sun behind her had not reached its apogee for the day. "We are proud of you."

"I'm not sure I know the way from here," I answered, my voice trailing off in partial defeat.

'You've been exceptional so far. Just remember to enjoy all the points along the way," she said so soothingly I wanted to believe her.

"Who are you?" I probed though I knew that question would go unanswered. The waves rushed in and escaped out, unleashing a new round of rolling rocks.

"There's no need for me to answer that. You already know." She started backing deeper into the surf. No matter how strong the waves were, they did not move her.

"But I don't," I said, my eyes pleading for her to tell me.

We stopped and stared at each other. Just then a monstrous wave approached the shore and lifted her into me.

I remained squatting on the boulder for I don't know how long—so paralyzing was my reverie. Eventually I arose and made my way back to civilization.

* * *

At the end of the summer and into the fall I embarked upon the pleasurable project of legally changing my name. First, with a carefully worded letter from my doctor, I petitioned the court to change my name to Maeve Chevonne

DuVally. Chevonne is Irish as well, but again I chose the anglicized spelling. Besides, I liked the fact each of my three names had a "v" in them.

Once the name change was approved, New York City required that a notice be run in a local newspaper. The publication of choice was the New York local paper for the Irish community, the *Irish Echo*. Given my name and heritage, this paper seemed appropriate, but it also made me laugh that this paper derived a steady revenue stream from trans people changing their names.

With a court-ordered name change and a doctor's note, I then replaced my name and gender marker on my Social Security card and driver's license. Once those were finished, everything else fell into place.

As the calendar moved into mid-fall, all the public engagements I had agreed to right after the *New York Times* story unfolded in rapid order. There were plenty of trans people who had come out before me in corporate America; but I had no doubt the Goldman Sachs name was what spawned the attention. To prevent the invitations and attention from going to my head, I constantly reminded myself I was being given this opportunity to use my public pulpit to help other people.

My first engagement at the women's diversity panel at a D.C. conference was mind-blowing. To have been invited to be on a stage with more well-known experts on diversity in front of a large audience felt electric. However, I felt distinctly out of my league answering questions about the biggest differences in the workplace I had experienced now being a woman compared to being a man. I didn't have enough experience to compare. All I had was my story, but over time I found that could take me a long way.

The business cable TV station CNBC also booked me to speak at a conference in front of a large audience with just me on stage. Wrapped in my favorite blush Theory dress and jacket, I was pumped, even though this format was not a great one for such an inexperienced speaker. I babbled for about ten minutes; after watching the clips of my performance, I rated it fair.

The fact that I could watch myself for ten minutes and rate it anything other than horrible was miraculous in of itself. Though the audience was 80 percent male, the only people who came up to compliment me after the talk were women. It wasn't true all the time, but I found that often cisgender, heterosexual men didn't know how to talk to me, so it was easier for them to avoid me. Women, by virtue of the power dynamic with men, could more easily identify with me.

Veronica Dagher, a reporter at the *Wall Street Journal*, who also did a podcast called "The Secrets of Wealthy Women," called one day asking me to come on and tell my coming out story, lessons learned, diversity in the workplace, and challenges for transgender people in the workplace. This was a new format for me and under the banner of the *Wall Street Journal*, it promised wide exposure.

But I was troubled again going in. For the same reason that the *New York Times* had come back to me days before publication, the story of my trans journey was missing something when I told it in the world. It lacked my alcoholism, which was a major element in the crucible from which Maeve was forged.

I told Veronica ahead of time I wanted to address my disease and recovery more directly and when she asked, I was ready with a crisp answer:

"I have had a long-standing drinking problem and a couple of years ago I decided to do something about that once and for all. In the aftermath of stopping drinking and the work that I did in terms of my recovery and getting to like myself better, I was given the gift, and I do consider it a gift, of knowing who I really am for the first time in my life."

Exiting the *Journal*'s offices and stepping into the bracing November chill of New York City, I walked toward the subway down Sixth Avenue to avoid the throngs milling in Times Square. Internally debating whether it was appropriate outing myself publicly as an alcoholic, I suddenly stopped and peered up at the skyscrapers surrounding me. I knew I had done the right thing because my motives were pure—to help other queer alcoholics and drug addicts. I did not know when the episode would air so I put it out of my mind and entered the subway at Forty-Second Street, plowing through the beggars and buskers.

In that instant, the goodness of the world pulsed a little longer and a little brighter than it had before.

ISLAND IN A RIVER

2020

NOW COMPLETELY OUT in all areas of my life, I was bursting with hope as 2020 dawned. I was scheduled to go to Costa Rica on March 14 with some sober friends, but the date of the trip was the week America woke up to the COVID-19 pandemic. At the start of the week, life and the trip seemed manageable, but by the end, though my flight left New York as scheduled, it would have been insane to be on it.

As opposed to the rest of the country, New York shut down quickly and I was suddenly leading a very solitary life, working from my small fourth-floor walk-up studio on the Upper East Side, only leaving to run early in the morning and buy groceries once or twice a week.

Everybody has their own story about their difficulties adjusting to this new reality, but for me, selfishly, it boiled down to two apprehensions. My gender affirmation surgery was scheduled for May 18 and as I watched elective surgeries being shut down by the governor of New York and death statistics mount, I felt certain my surgery would be postponed and uncertain when it would be rescheduled.

Additionally, the public speaking engagements that flooded my life, the new possibilities that opened, and the relationships I had developed in AA and work suddenly all seemed to wither. My world, which had appeared immense just weeks before, instantaneously deflated. AA meetings stopped over a two-week period in New York and slowly transitioned to online Zoom meetings.

I remember talking to my AA sponsor from a bench at the 90th Street entrance to Central Park on the East Side in mid-May.

"I'm in a really foul mood," I spit into the phone, so cross that I did not want to even discuss my feelings. At that moment, I didn't want to be more hopeful; I'd rather stew in misery. This was a throwback to the Michael days, but negativity is never eliminated. The best I could hope for was that it was less frequent and when it did appear, its presence fleeting.

The park was bursting with people of all ages and economic strata in masks, running, walking and biking. One older couple walking by me recoiled in horror when a group of teenagers without masks approached them.

"I can tell," my sponsor said with a slight degree of sarcasm.

"You know, I've been thinking. I derive my strength from being alone," I said though I knew it wasn't true as it was escaping from my mouth. Two men were arguing on the bridal path. Apparently, one had gotten too close to the other. The anger, fear and negativity of early COVID-19 in New York City belied the beauty of Central Park's flowering trees blooming to the point of exploding.

"That's not how most people experience it," my sponsor said somewhat charitably.

"Well, I'm not most people," I avowed, all the while becoming more incensed. And then I got to the real point. "It's not fair that I was planning to do all these things and I can't do them anymore."

"Now we're getting somewhere," my sponsor said, chuckling.

At the very start of COVID-19, I was despondent. For three days, I did my Goldman Sachs work from bed in the dark and tried to sleep as much as possible. I was quite sick at that time with COVID-19, I later found out. My flirtation with mild depression plagued me about a week and dissipated when I realized the big life I had was gone for the time being, but that didn't mean I couldn't create an alternative vast life for myself from my little New York apartment.

That is what I set out to do. I found a women's trans-friendly AA meeting in the city that I had never been to. For the first two months of quarantine, every day I tuned into this group's Zoom morning and evening meetings. For me, I had to replicate as much as I could the schedule I had before quarantine. That meant getting up and running at 5 a.m., showering and prettying myself for the morning AA meeting and then jumping right into my work.

Unless I arrived at Central Park early in the day and/or the weather was bad, it was too much of a hassle, especially with people challenging anybody who came too close. I took to running to the East River, passing the same spot where I had contemplated suicide two years before.

Gliding north along the river, I found a footbridge that took me over to Randalls and Wards Islands in the middle of the East River. I typically ran southeast along the far southern tip of Randalls Island, with grand views of the Upper East Side and Roosevelt Island. The wind was usually whipping one way or another. There were few people around at six in the morning but the sprouting tulips—yellow, red, white, and orange—kept me company.

My surgery was postponed but quickly rescheduled for June 3, meaning I was one of the first patients back on the docket when these procedures resumed at the start of June. In preparation for my physical recovery, I rented a temporary apartment for six weeks, because my own place was a fourth-floor walkup with fifty stairs, much too much for a newborn vagina. I moved in two days before my surgery and made sure I enjoyed my last extensive run for quite a while.

Starting at midday the day before my operation, I had to drink the bowel-cleansing gunk. This was not the liter bottle required for a colonoscopy but a full half-gallon of prescription-strength firewater. After consuming a third, I began to question its efficacy but just then the deluge began.

After a fitful night, I took a cab downtown to the hospital, a small specialty hospital called Manhattan Eye and Ear Infirmary where Mount Sinai did all its transgender surgeries. Skating through intake, I arrived at my room and changed into my gear—socks with grips, a frock, robe, mask and head covering. The hospital had only re-opened Monday and still felt like a mausoleum barely two days later. Slowly walking up to the toilet, I looked down at my penis, and let it empty me for the last time. Then I lay down to pray and meditate.

Around ten, I was sent down to a waiting room, which proved tedious because I had to leave my phone behind. Eventually, my surgeon, Dr. Pang, strode in, already bedecked in his scrubs.

"Are you all set?" he asked. A Hawaiian native, Dr. Pang was of Chinese descent and gay. Though reserved, whenever he spoke, it was eloquent.

"Yup, let's do it," I said. I had been waiting 58 years for this.

Somebody at Mount Sinai must have seen the *New York Times* story about me because Dr. Pang had been instructed to get a photo of us for promotional purposes. He didn't seem that enthusiastic but played along. "Are you okay taking a photo?"

"Sure. I don't feel very feminine in this," I said gesturing toward myself in the gender-neutral frock and head without a wig and makeup.

He smiled, took the selfie photo of the two of us and disappeared to prep.

Around 11:30, I was finally beckoned into the operating room. Up until then, the hospital had been quiet and wearisome but once I entered the OR, I was in an alien universe with flying saucer lights, music blaring and a half dozen or so nurses hustling around and chatting with intensity. I was hoping to get a warning when the anesthesia was about to be put into my IV bag so I could anticipate the rush just before passing out, but that never happened, and I felt myself losing consciousness.

I woke up to relief. Never again would I be plagued with something so wholly unwelcome. I didn't know what sex would look like going forward but it had to be better than what I had borne thus far in my life. I could still see the outline of my parts in my brain but there was no extension from my groin—only a sharp, steady pinch that was a constant reminder something had radically changed.

But it was not actually gone because my procedure was the popular penile inversion variety. My testicles were discarded but my penis and scrotum were repurposed for a higher cause—a vagina and clitoris. One of the doctors said he had never seen somebody come out of surgery so calmly. I simply opened my eyes, looked around and started asking questions about the nature of the pain and sensation I felt. The bottom of my feet ached for some reason. I had had that feeling when I was 20, back as an exchange student running in formation on the cold pavement as a member of the kenpo club at Kansai Gaidai. I lay in bed after the surgery feeling reborn, energized, content. I was now much closer to whom I was meant to be and could not wait to get back into the outside world. I called my sister Jennifer who had been by my side through all my tough times.

"I did it. No more peen, I got me a vag," I said, knowing I was smiling. The words poured out of my mouth like raging rapids. "I went to an AA meeting last night, but I think I scared the hell out of them," I said explaining that I'd not told most people in my group I was going in for surgery and just popped up in a Zoom meeting from a hospital bed.

"How are you feeling?" Jen asked, her vicarious excitement for me palpable.

"It's a bit sad not having anyone to visit me." I wanted to be positive. "I did get some flowers from a friend."

Pain free the rest of Wednesday and most of the day Thursday, I arrogantly concluded I had super strength to bury the discomfort that was supposed to come. By Thursday night, it arrived, making up for lost time. I subsequently discovered that one of the pain medications used during surgery was methadone, the effects of which lasted hours or even days after surgery. I shared an intimate and personal selfie of me propped up in bed with several dozen people through text. Everybody probably thought I was making the peace sign, but I was actually showing a "V" for vagina.

RECOVERY IN RECOVERY

2020

I WAS DISCHARGED FROM THE HOSPITAL after three nights, which I thought was a ridiculously short stay, given how intricate my surgery was, but that's the medical system we have. Attached to me were a catheter and a wound vacuum, which sucked liquid away from the surgical area. I lived in constant fear these devices would stop working and create some festering sore in my new vagina. Fortunately, I had a visiting nurse service for the first four weeks.

I asked Myla to spend time with me the first week and she stopped by every day, fetching me food from the store and the refrigerator. She would do anything for me, but I was careful not to talk about the vagina (which was a topic I could talk endlessly about and still can), because that was more information than she cared to know about.

I mostly just read, watched TV, took naps, and went to Zoom AA meetings. In other words, I gave myself permission to relax, something I usually was not very good at doing.

Flowers poured in, before my surgery, in the hospital right after my surgery and for the next month. The permutations were almost endless: roses only, meadow flowers, and bouquets in pink. The vases were placed on a mantel above a non-working fireplace right across the room from my bed. When I started feeling sorry for myself, I would just look at the flowers and my mood brightened.

How did my new anatomy make me feel? Just as taking anti-depressants after my last rock bottom in January of 2018 and female hormones in January of 2019, it elevated my mood and brought me closer to "feeling right."

One week after my surgery, I had my first follow-up appointment with Doctor Pang. Though I had heard some cis women strongly disliked stirrups, I was giddy resting my spread legs in them for the first time. As the doctor disconnected me from the catheter and the wound vac and took my dressing off, I looked down at what could only be described as a swollen bloody mess.

"It's not going to start looking normal for another couple of months," Dr. Pang said, obviously sensing my mood which he must have seen dozens of times previously. "And you won't really see the final shape for a year," he said, anticipating my next question.

"When can I start having sex?" I surprised myself by asking. I had no girlfriend and no prospects.

"After three months, you can begin to have penetrative sex," he said in his very methodical, clinical way. One of his surgical assistants was busy tapping notes on a computer nearby.

"We don't have to worry about that," I shot back and laughed.

Next came the instructions for dilating, which involved shoving a plastic rod up my vagina which needed to be held as deep as possible for a half hour. The pain was intense and stayed that way for weeks but gradually became almost tolerable over time.

Jackie and the boys came one afternoon, bringing flowers.

"How are you feeling?" Jackie asked through her mask. This visit was highly unusual in the world of COVID-19 in June of 2020. The case numbers in New York had peaked but were still very high and nobody really knew how contagious it was.

"The pain is manageable. It's too numb to hurt," I said, repeating the mantra I had decided on for the inevitable question. I had to lie as flat as possible to take excess pressure off my butt which, in turn, would have been relayed to my front.

Jackie arched her eyebrow, surprised.

"Then I get these sharp pains which the doctor says are nerve endings reattaching," I added, knowing this sounded weighty and interesting.

Connor was walking around the apartment, inspecting the kitchen, bathroom, and balcony. "It's cool," he said. He had always prided himself on rating the various hotel rooms and summer rentals we had stayed in over the years.

"You look pretty good for two weeks," Jackie observed. The door to the balcony was open and the scents of grilled Italian sausage wafted into the room.

"I have a high tolerance for suffering, and I heal well. Clean living," I said, and we laughed. I wondered what if I hadn't had a drinking problem but still had my trans realization when I did? Would Jackie have stayed with me? I dismissed the question because the answer was unknowable.

"The doctor said if I heal well, I might be able to go to Cape Cod for my third month of convalescence," I exclaimed, showing my excitement by propping myself up only to slide back after realizing I wasn't supposed to be doing that. "We'll have to see."

Whenever I talked about Cape Cod, I hoped Jackie might bite and say she wanted to go, or she remembered the good times we had there when we vacationed with the boys. She never did. Between all the packing she was responsible for and me sneaking drinks whenever I could, I don't think she had many fond memories. There was nothing surprising in this visit. We remained close and genuinely cared about each other. Anything that reeked of intimacy was off limits though, just as any detailed discussion of my new anatomy was.

I left the house for walks around the bridal path in Central Park at four weeks, brisk marches at five weeks and slow lopes at six weeks. For some reason, that summer I found listening to Crosby, Stills and Nash very soothing. At five weeks, my doctor said I was healing nicely, and I could go to Cape Cod for the third month of my three-month leave from Goldman Sachs. I was able to snag a place in Truro, right next to Wellfleet where our good friends Ed and Gordon owned a beautiful white house steeped in oyster history.

I invited three friends, Laura, Joanne and Jessica, for the first of four weeks I would be staying there. Fully out for more than a year, I was making friends with more women. We played cards, cooked together, went to the beach and hung around in Provincetown. This was an important summer for me to be up by P-town because during the first part of my transition I was so focused on myself I hadn't given much thought to the fact that I was part of something bigger—the entire LGBTQ+ community.

I always thought the freshwater ponds of the Cape were an underappreciated natural asset. These kettle ponds had formed when bits of ice fell of the retreating glacier during the Ice Age, carving out depressions that filled with water over time.

While Wellfleet has larger and better-known ponds, Truro has a few of its own. Exploring the area around our rental, we discovered Snow Pond, right off the main Route Six drag. From our parked car, the four of us clambered down a gentle hill, which rolled into the little sandy beach everybody used to enter the pond. It was almost round, encircled by a combination of evergreens and deciduous trees, which made this, and all the other ponds nearby, feel very private. There were lily pads and some pond grass on the far side and a white buoy floating in the exact middle.

We went late in the day because Jessica had an aversion to the sun. I didn't. My new body craved its heat as a form of nourishment. Most of the edges of the pond were already in shadow but long rays from the sinking sun still caressed the little beach. Jessica had previously made it clear that there would be no clothes here and fortunately no other visitors had appeared.

My shorts and skimpy blouse were off in a second and I turned to face my friends. They were all looking at my pubis and nodding which caused me to break into an ear-touching grin. Even though my bits were still messy, Dr. Pang's skill was clear to these cisgender women.

Not wanting to be too much of an exhibitionist, I plunged through the tranquil surface of the water and headed toward the buoy using my best crawl stroke. The water tickled my labia, and I realized the bottom of my naked swimming body was sleeker because there was no penis acting as a rudder. Jessica followed me out as Joanne and Laura splashed closer to shore.

Back on the beach, it seemed a shame to cover up. Drying off while wandering down a path that went off into the woods, I was Eve for a moment before returning to reality. I didn't so much want to flaunt my naked body but rather just be out in the world with it. Reluctantly, I acquiesced to society's prudishness.

Now that everybody had seen the handiwork, I talked about it at every turn, including updates on my nocturnal experimentation. One morning I came down from my bedroom with a long face.

"What's wrong?" Jessica asked.

"I can't orgasm," I mumbled, looking away. "I can get to the middle part but not from there to the final part."

Jessica blurted out, "Welcome to being a woman."

That night it happened, and I came bounding down the stairs the next morning and announced my success to my three new friends with a great big grin. "I'm clitorally orgasmic." I don't even know if that is a term anybody besides me used, but it seemed like the right thing to say.

A couple of nights after we had all settled in, there was a full moon and everybody except me seemed to know that it was important to do a full moon ritual. Joanne and Laura wanted to stay close to the rental, but Jessica insisted we go find one of the beaches and look up into the night sky. It was maybe 10 or 11 at night and I didn't yet know the geography of all the Truro bayside beaches. Finally, I turned onto a road that cut through dune grass and led out to a modest beach. The small waves gently slapped the shore, and a tender breeze stroked our faces as we picked up our blanket and laid it out on the sand.

Jessica, charismatic with a curly mop of brown hair, showed me an app on her iPhone that identified celestial bodies when the smart phone was pointed upward. Saturn and Jupiter happened to be quite visible, which excited me. With difficulty because of periodic gusts, we lit a couple of candles and placed them beside the blanket anchored in the Cape Cod sand. Jessica, her porcelain-white skin reflecting the moonlight, and I lay down, side by side touching in some places, which was warm and soothing.

I smiled inside and out, setting my intentions for the full moon: fortitude to immerse myself in writing; fortune to experience intimacy in my new body; and resolve to leave Goldman Sachs when the time was right.

How was the fine thread of Maeve, interwoven through

my life, tethered to this moment? The thread had encircled me again and again; next, a metamorphosis occurred. When the cocoon casing fell away, I was gender enlightened. From there, the path forward was clear, and I set off without hesitation, knowing who I was and the ecstasy that comes with that.

At this moment, I was here, with a small knot of women who accepted and loved me as one of theirs. This was a place where I was meant to be; it was bright, weightless, and easy—everything my life *before Maeve* was not. All along it was as simple as knowing who I was and living in harmony with that self. Simple, yet so arduous as to have been unattainable.

Until it was—and then all else became possible. Maybe this is just what it feels like to love myself.

BACK TO JAPAN, FINALLY

2022

IF THE GENDER AWAKENING was my Big Bang, the pieces of me continued to get reconfigured and my universe to expand exponentially. At the end of 2021, friends from my Japan days thirty-five years ago began copying me on emails regarding the possibility of a reunion of the teachers on the government teaching program that had brought me to Kumamoto. The tentative timetable, March 2022, came and went, sabotaged by COVID-19 but a new date was set for November of the same year.

Returning to Japan for first time since 1992 became an obsession. Though I made travel reservations, the trip remained in doubt as of early summer because Japan was not yet open to the outside world. My yearning, long dormant, to return to the country that helped shape me, welled up. In the meantime, in June 2022, I left Goldman Sachs after 18 years with my head held high and the promise of consulting work that would keep me connected to the institution that had been such a large part of my life for the last two decades.

As the summer progressed, Japan opened up in stages, but it was not until late September that a date for a full reopening was set—October 11. The timing was fortuitous because the reunion was scheduled for November 4-6 and my flight was booked for November 2. I feverishly began constructing a trip spanning three weeks that traversed three separate regions and tried to pack in as much nostalgia and fresh experiences as possible. Of course, one goal was to fashion something exceptional to unleash Maeve's femininity, which had effervesced to the surface during my Japan years but was never fully realized there.

My United flight, mostly purchased with a credit from my unfulfilled Costa Rica trip of March 2020, landed in Narita Airport on the afternoon of November 3, exactly 30 years since I had last stepped foot in the country. Upon disembarking, I was ushered through a vast web of COVID-19 checkpoints. My first surprise was that non-Japanese occupied some of the roles at those checkpoints, something unthinkable three decades earlier. I knew the trip would be a combination of the familiar and unfamiliar, but there was no way of predicting which would appear when. I soon noticed that the fluidity of my Japanese and the ability to construct sentences was still intact, but my vocabulary had atrophied.

Checking in to a hotel close to the airport in Chiba, within two hours of my landing I found the earthen embankment of a nearby river to run on. As I did whenever I jogged in a place I was visiting, I honored the earth upon which my destination was built. After a dinner of curry rice, I had my only transgender misunderstanding during the entire trip. Some overzealous hotel employees tried to herd me to the male side of a hotel spa, which I resisted and then burst through the threshold of the female side.

The next day I took the bullet train to Kobe in the Kansai

region where the reunion was to be held. The train's speed and sleekness awed me just as it had decades earlier. Like every other tourist, I gawked as we passed Mount Fuji in the distance. Near the end of the journey, the train zipped past Hirakata and I conjured the ghosts of young Atchan and pre-Maeve sitting on benches getting to know each other.

The gathering was effectively my reintroduction to Japan and allowed me to begin the process of connecting my new sober, girl-self to a time in my life that I was a much different person. The ending boat ride down an untamed river in Kyoto suited my mood; I felt wild and wanted to run free through the country. That Sunday, I checked into the Kyoto inn where I would be staying for four nights, barely able to contain my excitement. The old capital of Japan, Kyoto is jammed with palaces, shrines, temples, and lush, sculptured gardens. Kyoto was less than an hour away by train and I had traveled there several times as an exchange student, but I had never stayed long.

My quarters, a beautiful inn-style hotel with a timber front that resembled structures from centuries ago, only enhanced the charm of my experience in Kyoto. The Japanese people revere their past, but the locations that preserved that history had dwindled due to the modernization and urbanization of the country. Of all the places in Japan, Kyoto retained its bond with antiquity. The inn's bathing facility was another perk, housing the equivalent of a public bath with clean gray surfaces and a hot, serene bath that erased both weariness and grime.

In public locker rooms and bathing areas, I had been very modest, trying to blend in and not offend the women present. But after the Chiba anti-trans experience, I generously flashed my boobs and nether parts to show I belonged. Rounding out the experience, the Japanese breakfast that was served included steaming rice, sour Japanese pickles, various forms of tofu and miso soup. I would die healthy and happy if I was so fortunate to eat such a simple feast every day.

I had been in Japan for four days and was finally on my own. The first order of business the next morning was to find a prime running spot, which I did. The Kamo River bisects the city and stretches for miles and miles into the distant mountains. Later in the day I wandered Gion, Kyoto's old section where geisha can still be seen. I didn't bump into any, but I saw many Japanese women old and young in vibrant *kimonos* stylishly walking, knowing they were turning heads and connecting to Japan's past.

I shopped for Japanese trinkets that would make thoughtful Christmas stocking stuffers for my children and Jackie and sampled the local fare that I remembered, particularly the cabbage pancakes, *okonomiyaki*.

A year earlier, I had ended a post-operation fling spanning two summers with Jessica, the vivacious bisexual woman who swam naked by my side in the Cape Cod ponds. It was the first relationship in my new body and in sobriety. I slathered it with an intimacy I had not experienced in years given my alcoholism had long ago stolen any vestiges of that from my marriage to Jackie. There were times, especially during the first summer of the new connection, when my face hurt from smiling every waking hour. Sadly, we were incompatible for the long term, and the end of the union devastated me for months. But resiliency is not something I lack.

At week's end, I bade farewell to beautiful Kyoto and headed to Kumamoto, where I had visited middle and high schools in the mid-1980s. Kumamoto's main airport nearly abuts the ancient caldera of Mount Aso, which still loomed large in my imagination. I transferred to a puddle jumper for a short flight to Amakusa, Kumamoto's western fishing peninsula.

Over the last couple of years, I became fascinated with a

remote Amakusa fishing village that had a still functioning church and a 400-year history with Catholicism imported by Portuguese missionaries. Studying the village and church through photographs wasn't good enough. I had planned my three-week Japanese trip meticulously, but logistics around getting to and from Sakitsu Village were a bit sketchy due to the lack of information and remoteness. When I contacted the owner of the house where I was staying for two nights, Mr. Nakata, he informed me there was no way to get there via public transit, but he offered to drive me back and forth to the airport.

To call the village far flung and isolated was litotes. Besides fishing, it lacked any form of commerce. There was a small general store where the shopkeeper could often be found dozing on the *tatami* mat at the back; and an Italian restaurant, which had a limited, albeit delicious, menu. For the 48 hours I was there, my menu largely consisted of instant ramen, Japanese tangerines and Pocky, the Japanese treat of slim biscuit sticks dunked in chocolate.

In the morning, I ran along the coastline through two other small fishing villages and climbed a small mountain that gave me panoramic views of the East China Sea, which fashioned stunning sunsets at the end of the day. After showering, I ate at the one restaurant by appointment, and walked into Sakitsu church. It was Catholic but with a Japanese flavor—the floor was mostly covered in *tatami* mats. Sitting on the fragrant dried rush, I propped myself against a pillar and gulped the trappings of the church. Secure now in myself, a church could never hurt me again.

I next mounted a hill to the town's shrine and viewed the church through a Shinto lens. The gratifying day ended with a hike to the other side of the harbor to take in still another vantage point.

The next day I was in Kumamoto City where I had lived during my time in the prefecture. There I purchased one big material gift from the trip to myself, a pink-tinged pearl necklace. Because my homestay parents were not up for a visit, I was in Kumamoto City for no other reason than I had been there before. Walking the covered mall areas and popping into restaurants and shops, I had hours to engage in reflection about the important people in my life. Despite the destruction and collateral damage I had left in my wake, I had cordial, warm and respectful relationships with my two former wives, Michi and Jackie. That was more a testament to their generosity than my efforts. My bond with Myla, given all we had shared, continued to deepen. Liam, now a budding adult, and I had developed a fondness and admiration for each other. Steeping in his teenage years, Connor and I didn't maintain constant closeness but there were moments that gave me hope.

For my extended family, my youngest sister Jennifer, whom I had not been particularly close to in early life, had become my dearest confidante. Though she lived in Los Angeles, we are both queer and she had the same type of spirituality and outlook on life. I could tell her anything. My two brothers and Deirdre accepted me completely, mainly because they recognized how happy I was as Maeve. My mother's memory was already in deep fade when I came out, but I once made a joke in front of her about being a "hot chick" and she smirked. Perhaps, some part of her knew Maeve. Would my father have accepted me had he been alive when I came out. Who the hell knows?

I am so fortunate.

During the Kyoto and Kumamoto parts of my trip, I spent a good deal of time alone. By the time I arrived in Tokyo for the last eight days of my Japan sojourn, I craved human interaction, which still surprised me given how much of a loner I had been for most of my life. I now regarded myself as a shy extrovert.

The first particular on my agenda was a visit to Yokohama to see Atchan, my first love who I hadn't laid eyes on in 37 years. We met at her local train station and took a bus to an udon restaurant she liked. We started to reacquaint ourselves with one another between loud slurps of the thick white noodles.

Now married with two adult children, she filled her small apartment with her musician husband's equipment and her English teaching materials strewn over the kitchen table. Her family was embroiled in lawsuits with an overzealous neighbor, she explained. There was a lot of context, much of which became evident in a film her son had made about the dispute. Our spirits began to rejoin during the viewing.

"I spend most of my time preparing for court hearings," she explained. Her hair was streaked with gray, and she no longer dressed in surfer wear but the essence of the girl I knew from over three decades ago still emanated.

"Come visit me in New York when that's over," I gently beseeched. I wanted to see her outside of the domestic habitat she had brought me to.

"Now that my mother is dead, I don't go anywhere," she said, with her back to me as she dropped vegetables and *tofu* into a boiling pot to make a kind of vegetarian *sukiyaki* on my account. "This town has everything I need."

As we ate the stew, I teased, "Is this the first time you've cooked this year?" Domesticity had never been her forte.

I appreciated her effort in preparing a meal though her daughter termed it "slop" and not fit for a guest when she popped into the apartment.

I played her a recording of an audio magazine article about my life. We were quiet after it was over. Though my story has a happy ending, even people who knew me well through the years were surprised at its darkness.

"I didn't know you were so sad. I'm sorry," she said, looking into my eyes. I held her stare and for that moment we were back in her Providence dorm room divulging to each other our life hopes and ambitions.

Uncomfortable staying in this moment for too long, I broke the silence, explaining, "I want you to know you made my life happier and better."

I had not planned to stay over but she was insistent, and I had nothing planned my second night in Tokyo. At midnight, almost twelve hours after we had first sat down at the table to catch up, we bade each other good night and I crawled into my guest futon for a fitful sleep. We would not see each other often in the future, but she was now a part of my life again.

* * *

And then, Goldman Sachs took over. Masa-san, a senior executive and outspoken Japanese gay activist, and others made sure I found the engagement I desired. My last Friday in Japan was Pink Day, a corporate recognition day for LGBTQ+ people in Asia. In honor of Pink Day, I spoke at Goldman Sachs and at several clients' offices. Trudging all over Tokyo from my hotel to meet clients with Masa-san was exhilarating and felt like I was replicating in Tokyo the kind of life I had back in New York.

On the evening of Pink Day, Masa-san and I dined on traditional Japanese Buddhist vegetarian food and then we headed to Shinjuku Ni-Chome, the gay district where I met my first wife. Joining forces with a trans woman I had been introduced to, Tiffany, and a prominent trans activist whom I had wanted to meet, we first tried a club full of young foreigners getting drunk. It was particularly unappealing, but I suspected that was because it reminded me of myself 35 years earlier.

Smiling, Masa-san said, "I know a place."

Housed in an unexceptional five-story building, our destination was one of a half-dozen drinking spots behind a dull aluminum veneer—each one having its own flavor. Our creaky, claustrophobic elevator opened onto a floor with a darkened bar about the size of a master bedroom. We walked into the tasteful space, which had perhaps six seats around the bar and then couch-like seating for another half dozen guests along the back wall, which was covered in a deep red velvet.

"You have to be invited to come here," Masa-san explained.

I turned behind me to observe a sign on the wall in Japanese and English that read each group of men could have no more than one woman in their party. One of the Japanese men sitting next to me suddenly stood up, walked over to the bar, lifted the hinged arm and sat down to a piano I had not even noticed. From nowhere, the well-groomed bearded bartender with the sleek black vest and bow tie pulled a full bass up from under the bar and started jamming to a jazz tune with the piano-playing customer.

Masa-san and the trans activist Fumino-san were engrossed in conversation while Tiffany and I, sipping our sparkling waters, soaked in the unbridled joy of the drinking establishment where these men were fully accepted and could let down the façade that Japan requires for all its people, particularly those who do not conform to the majority profile. Before I made this trip, I had said one of my goals was to experience how it felt to be queer in Japan. This bar filled in the picture for me. Though the challenges and slights would be different here than in the U.S., I could be a joyful out transgender woman in Tokyo, if I chose to live there.

Every day there had been a joyful celebration of life and the turn mine had taken five years before. Trips like this are not common.

Momentarily lost in the fullness of my life, I focused and reset my intentions: For my family, to try to make up for the past; and, to continue to sponsor and mentor alcoholics, addicts, trans people and any other queers who needed help. I aspired to carry on being a benevolent, generous human being who keeps my tiny corner of the universe as sparkling clean as possible.

I realized that I hadn't just become Maeve. I had to keep becoming Maeve every tick of my life because she is not only an actual being, but also an idealized terminus that I would never reach. But the nobility of striving and struggling to touch something ultimately untouchable inspires me to seek and ultimately infuses my life with transcendent value.

Spiritual economics rule in the universe. As I saw virtually all my deepest wishes coming to pass, I now know the more I am in service to the world, the more enriched my life becomes.

It's time to dream bigger.

EPILOGUE

MY TIME IN JAPAN was one of the most memorable experiences I've ever had but I left something out.

About a half year before my trip, my old Japan friend Timothy had introduced me to the generous Filipina trans woman Tiffany from the gay bar who had a podcast, "Breakfast with Tiffany." Invited on as a guest, I found the conversation so compelling—my earlier time in Japan and my U.S. trans experience—the time difference, which dictated an 11 p.m. start on my end, didn't bother me at all. Tiffany also had a side gig helping foreigners who could afford it touch Japan in more personal ways than the average tourist could. She had both off-the-shelf explorations but would also design something exceptionally unique if requested.

Ever since my gender awakening in 2018, I yearned to be wrapped in a *kimono* and photographed by a professional photographer in glorious Kyoto settings. When I realized my Japan trip would happen, I tasked Tiffany with actualizing my dream. She set about orchestrating what she called Maeve's *Kimono* Adventure.

Originally, I had requested that Tiffany arrange for me to be dressed as a geisha replete with white makeup and a wig.

She convinced me this would be disrespectful to the culture and assured me that with what she had planned, I was going to be very satisfied. Besides, I had not transformed myself into a proud, confident woman to serve men as the geisha did.

At last, my *kimono* day dawned. After a quick run and dip in the Kyoto inn's public bath, I joined Tiffany in a cab to Gion. She had rented *kimonos* in Tokyo in the color schemes I desired—heavy on pink. The price of the adventure was not cheap, and I had added significantly to it by requesting a midday change into a second *kimono*. This was a fantasy dream, and I was not about to skimp.

We arrived at the studio on the outskirts of Gion—a place where modern-day geisha and other women in the so-called water trade (high-end drinking establishments) came to be dressed and made up.

I sat in a chair in front of a mirror and waited to be transformed. A young hairdresser put my hair up tight around my head and fastened it in place with a dozen bobby pins and what seemed to be a full aerosol can of hairspray. Next, a young woman painted my face, drawing out and accenting my best features in a way I had never before experienced. Then we retired to a back room with *tatami* mats and big mirrors for the last, but perhaps most important piece of the artwork, the *kimono*.

First, swathes of soft cotton were draped over my shoulder, and then an undergarment slipped over my body and held in place with tightened sashes. Finally, the sumptuous silk Japanese gown of black with pink cherry blossoms was slipped on. As I gazed at the mirror mesmerized, the attendant began the intricate process of tying my pink and light blue obi. The finishing touch was brightly colored and festive hair ornaments. Too happy to smile, I continued to stare at myself in disbelief. I had never looked or felt so feminine.

This is what I was meant to be.

We walked amongst the temples and shrines, mostly places like Heian Shrine, which were not normally top tourist destinations. Tiffany and a friend of hers, a Filipino photographer, directed me where to stand, sit, move, and hold a traditional waxed paper umbrella.

When I was too stiff, Tiffany, herself an experienced model, showed me how to relax. Other tourists stopped and watched, wondering if I was well known in any way. Ever the concerned hostess, Tiffany constantly asked if I was tired. Literally hundreds of photos had been snapped, but how could I grow tired of looking beautiful and sharing my exquisiteness with others? I wanted to do this every day for the rest of my life.

When I looked at some of the photos, though I am clearly non-Asian, the serene, content expression on my face made me wonder if I were Japanese in a past life. Maybe my supposed whim to go to Japan in the first place was not capriciousness after all?

Early in the afternoon we returned to the studio, and I changed to a pink *kimono* circled by a crimson and turmeric *obi*. The afternoon theme was ponds in Japanese gardens with the photographer trying to capture double Maeves through water reflections. Although the *kimono* was cinched tight against my upper body and restricted leg movement, the elegance felt like freedom. Not knowing when I would do this again, I felt sadness when stripping off the opulence, and dull in my Western street clothes.

Tiffany and I went out to a tempura bar that night and conversed with the chef as he fried vegetables and fish right in front of us one at a time. As I lay down for the night, I wondered how to process a day I had been dreaming about for five years. The purest form of bliss, it could only be enhanced by one addition—sharing the experience with a girlfriend.

I will be back.

Enjoy more about
Maeve Rising
Meet the Author
Check out author appearances
Explore special features

MAEVE CHEVONNE DUVALLY

Maeve is a multicultural communications specialist, storyteller and LGBTQ+ advocate. She has spent the bulk of her career as a journalist and corporate spokesperson, most recently at Goldman Sachs.

After a lifetime of working for large companies, she is forging her own path, now consulting for corporations and other entities on communications strategy and diversity, equity and inclusion. Maeve also mentors transgender people and is a frequent public speaker on LGBTQ+ workplace issues.

She was a managing director in corporate communications at Goldman Sachs over an 18-year career. Prior to joining Goldman, Maeve worked in media relations at Merrill Lynch.

Before that, she was a financial journalist and editor at Bridge News for nearly 15 years with stints in Tokyo, Washington D.C. and New York. She spent ten formative years in Japan in the 1980s and is fluent in the language.

Maeve serves on the boards of GLAAD; the Knight-Bagehot Fellowship, a journalism non-profit; Connecticut-based LGBTQ+ health provider Anchor Health Initiative; and Trans New York.

She earned a B.A. in English from Providence College in 1983 and was a Knight-Bagehot Fellow at Columbia University Graduate School of Journalism School in 1994.

ACKNOWLEDGEMENTS

I would like to thank the Diversity and Inclusion team at Goldman Sachs, particularly Lisa Douglas, for making my public coming out so meaningful. Also, my gratitude goes out to Emily Flitter of the *New York Times*, whose sensitive portrayal of my experience taught me the true power of storytelling.

I am eternally indebted to Tiffany Rossdale, who arranged the kimono photoshoot described in the Epilogue. One of the best days of my life, it continues to inspire me.

My appreciation also goes out to Vicki DeArmon, Julia Park Tracey and the rest of the team at Sibylline Press who believed in my story.

And lastly, I would be remiss in not calling out my family members—Jackie, Michi, Myla, Liam, Connor, Deirdre, John-Peter, Jennifer, and Ryan—for their unwavering support.

—Maeve DuVally

BOOK GROUP QUESTIONS

Maeve Rising: Coming Out Trans in Corporate America
by Maeve DuVally

1. Maeve experienced a lot of trauma at the hands of her parents and in her upbringing. What elements of her early life did you think contributed to her alcoholism?

2. How does Maeve's midlife realization that she was a woman show up for her in earlier decades? In what way did the culture of the 1980s, for example, allow her to explore androgyny or gender in ways that other decades did not support?

3. How does visiting and living in Japan affect Maeve's sense of self? Explore her time in Japan and how it helped shape Maeve's sexual exploration, substance abuse, and self-esteem.

4. Maeve gets quite explicit in describing her body metamorphosis. How did you react to reading these descriptions: fascinated, curious, grateful for the knowledge?

5. What is your experience in working with trans women and men? Have you met people who use other pronouns than what you expected? Have you had to learn a new name for someone in your family, school or work environment? What is the hardest aspect of a person's gender reveal for you, the acquaintance or outsider? How do you think the person themselves feels?

6. Did it surprise you that Goldman Sachs was so accommodating to Maeve's reveal? What were some aspects about the employment reveal that surprised or impressed you?

7. Which do you think would be more challenging to deal with as a spouse, a parent, a child, or a fellow employee: a person's severe addiction and subsequent sobriety or a person's body dysphoria and subsequent metamorphosis?

Sibylline

PRESS

Sibylline Press is proud to publish the brilliant work of women authors over 50. We are a woman-owned publishing company and, like our authors, represent women of a certain age. In our first season we have three outstanding fiction (historical fiction and mystery) and three incredible memoirs to share with readers of all ages.

HISTORICAL FICTION

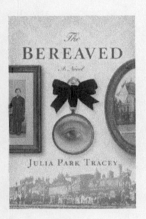

The Bereaved: A Novel
By Julia Park Tracey

Paperback ISBN: 978-1-7367954-2-2
5 3/8 x 8 3/4 | 274 pages | $18
ePub ISBN: 978-1-9605730-0-1 | $12.60

Based on the author's research into her grandfather's past as an adopted child, and the surprising discovery of his family of origin and how he came to be adopted, Julia Park Tracey has created a mesmerizing work of historical fiction illuminating the darkest side of the Orphan Train.

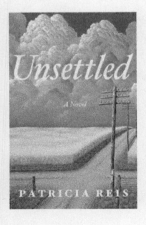

Unsettled: A Novel
By Patricia Reis

Paperback ISBN: 978-1-7367954-8-4
5 3/8 x 8 3/4 | 378 pages | $19
ePUB ISBN: 978-1-960573-05-6 | $13.30

In this lyrical historical fiction with alternating points of view, a repressed woman begins an ancestral quest through the prairies of Iowa, awakening family secrets and herself, while in the late 1800s, a repressed ancestor, Tante Kate, creates those secrets.

MYSTERY

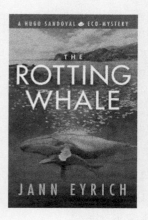

The Rotting Whale: A Hugo Sandoval Eco-Mystery
By Jann Eyrich

Paperback ISBN: 978-1-7367954-3-9
5 3/8 x 8 3/8 | 212 pages | $17
ePub ISBN: 978-1-960573-03-2 | $11.90

In this first case in the new Hugo Sandoval Eco-Mystery series, an old-school San Francisco building inspector with his trademark Borsalino fedora, must reluctantly venture outside his beloved city and find his sea legs before he can solve the mystery of how a 90-ton blue whale became stranded, twice, in a remote inlet off the North Coast.

MORE TITLES IN THIS ECO-MYSTERY SERIES TO COME:
Spring '24: *The Blind Key* | ISBN: 978-1-7367954-5-3
Fall '24: *The Singing Lighthouse* | ISBN: 978-1-7367954-6-0

MEMOIR

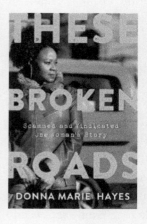

These Broken Roads: Scammed and Vindicated, One Woman's Story
By Donna Marie Hayes

Tradepaper ISBN: 978-1-7367954-4-6
5 3/8 x 8 3/8 | 226 pages | $17
ePUB ISBN: 978-1-960573-04-9 | $11.90

In this gripping and honest memoir, Jamaican immigrant Donna Marie Hayes recounts how at the peak of her American success in New York City, she is scammed and robbed of her life's savings by the "love of her life" met on an online dating site and how she vindicates herself to overcome a lifetime of bad choices.

MEMOIR *(cont.)*

Maeve Rising: Coming Out Trans in Corporate America
By Maeve DuVally

Paperback ISBN: 978-1-7367954-1-5
5 3/8 x 8 3/8 | 284 pages | $18
ePub ISBN: 978-1-960573-01-8 | $12.60

In this searingly honest LBGQT+ memoir, Maeve DuVally tells the story of coming out transgender in one of the most high-profile financial institutions in America, Goldman Sachs.

Reading Jane: A Daughter's Memoir
By Susannah Kennedy

Paperback ISBN: 978-1-7367954-7-7
5 3/8 x 8 3/8 | 306 pages | $19
ePub ISBN: 978-1-960573-02-5 | $13.30

After the calculated suicide of her domineering and narcissistic mother, Susannah Kennedy grapples with the ties between mothers and daughters and the choices parents make in this gripping memoir that shows what freedom looks like when we choose to examine the uncomfortable past.

Sibylline
PRESS

For more information about Sibylline Press and our authors, please visit us at **www.sibyllinepress.com**